THE
MOTIVATED
BRAIN

ASCD MEMBER BOOK

Many ASCD members received this book as a
member benefit upon its initial release.

Learn more at: **www.ascd.org/memberbooks**

Gayle **GREGORY**   Martha **KAUFELDT**

THE
MOTIVATED
BRAIN

Improving Student Attention, Engagement, and Perseverance

Alexandria, Virginia USA

1703 N. Beauregard St. • Alexandria, VA 22311-1714 USA
Phone: 800-933-2723 or 703-578-9600 • Fax: 703-575-5400
Website: www.ascd.org • E-mail: member@ascd.org
Author guidelines: www.ascd.org/write

Deborah S. Delisle, *Executive Director;* Stefani Roth, *Publisher;* Genny Ostertag, *Director, Content Acquisitions;* Allison Scott, *Acquisitions Editor;* Julie Houtz, *Director, Book Editing & Production;* Deborah Siegel, *Editor;* Georgia Park, *Senior Graphic Designer;* Mike Kalyan, *Manager, Production Services;* Keith Demmons, *Production Designer;* Andrea Wilson, *Senior Production Specialist*

All referenced trademarks are the property of their respective owners.

All web links in this book are correct as of the publication date below but may have become inactive or otherwise modified since that time. If you notice a deactivated or changed link, please e-mail books@ascd.org with the words "Link Update" in the subject line. In your message, please specify the web link, the book title, and the page number on which the link appears.

PAPERBACK ISBN: 978-1-4166-2048-8 ASCD product # 115041
PDF E-BOOK ISBN: 978-1-4166-2054-9 see Books in Print for other formats.
Quantity discounts: 10–49, 10%; 50+, 15%; 1,000+, special discounts (e-mail programteam@ascd.org or call 800-933-2723, ext. 5773, or 703-575-5773). For desk copies, go to www.ascd.org/desk-copy.

ASCD Member Book No. FY16-1A (Sep. 2015 PSI+). ASCD Member Books mail to Premium (P), Select (S), and Institutional Plus (I+) members on this schedule: Jan, PSI+; Feb, P; Apr, PSI+; May, P; Jul, PSI+; Aug, P; Sep, PSI+; Nov, PSI+; Dec, P. For current details on membership, see www.ascd.org/membership.

Library of Congress Cataloging-in-Publication Data
Gregory, Gayle.
   The motivated brain : improving student attention, engagement, and perseverance / Gayle Gregory, Martha Kaufeldt.
      pages cm
   ASCD Member Book No. FY16-1A (September 2015 PSI+)
   Includes bibliographical references and index.
   ISBN 978-1-4166-2048-8 (pbk. : alk. paper) 1. Motivation in education. 2. Learning, Psychology of. 3. Learning--Physiological aspects. I. Kaufeldt, Martha, 1954- II. Title.
   LB1065.G74 2015
   370.15'4--dc23
                         2015011011

23 22 21 20 19 18 17 16 15   1 2 3 4 5 6 7 8 9 10 11 12

THE
MOTIVATED
BRAIN

Improving Student Attention, Engagement, and Perseverance

Foreword

Perspectives on Our Emotional Nature and Implications for Educational Advances

Gregory and Kaufeldt superbly summarize the implication of our ever-increasing scientific understanding about our fundamental emotional nature on the development of better educational practices. The affective neuroscientific understanding of animal emotionality has helped illuminate some of the greatest mysteries of human existence— the basic psychological forces that motivate people, both young and old, to behave in characteristic ways (Panksepp, 1998; Panksepp & Biven, 2012). Indeed, our personality structures reflect the strengths and weaknesses of our various affective strengths and weakness, mental powers that we share in kind, if not precise detail, with other mammals. In medicine we have learned the underlying principles by which human bodies operate through detailed studies of animal bodies. In education, the neuroscientific understanding of our affective minds will help inform and refine our instructional practices. Furthering that understanding is the great achievement of this book.

   Our brains' basic affective functions—"evolutionary memories"— enhance our capacity to *anticipate* survival issues. Through learning, our brains promote knowledge of the world. It is important for educators to understand such foundations of human minds, and how they can inform development of new educational practices.

The fundamental importance of our children's affective lives is superbly illuminated in this book. Surprisingly, this possibility has emerged substantially because of our increasing knowledge about the minds of other animals, especially the diverse attentional, emotional, and motivational systems that constitute the core of organismic psychological coherence. As we better appreciate the emotional "tools for living" built into all mammalian brains, we can enhance educational experiences for all children. We must obviously minimize the negative affective forces of FEAR (anxiety), RAGE (anger), and PANIC (separation-distress/psychological-pain/loneliness systems), but with that work done, we must amplify the diverse intellectual riches that only a full engagement of the SEEKING system can provide—the massive emotional-motivational system that supports our urges to PLAY with and CARE for others, not to mention the turmoil of LUST emerging in adolescence. An understanding of these systems tells us much about where we should be going in our educational processes. This book clarifies important dimensions of human existence, while drawing out didactic implications.

Thus, this text offers a clear understanding of our emotional nature and how that beneficially affects educational practices. It is among the first to consider the spectra of wisdom emerging from ongoing neuroscientific inquiries: we are born emotional creatures. Child-rearing practices that respect this are already providing superlative guidelines for improving child development (Sunderland, 2006).

This book introduces educators to our fundamental emotional processes that come at various levels of complexity within the bottom-up hierarchical structures of mental development, that eventually, with normal maturation and education, allow children healthy top-down regulation of their urges. Among the brain's emotional networks, the SEEKING system—long inappropriately called "The Brain Reward System" (in fact, there are many rewarding systems in the brain)—is the one that deserves the greatest emphasis in education. Being the foundation for healthy exploration, with feelings of enthusiasm and curiosity, understanding this system is critical for students to become active learners.

Because it mediates so many important functions of the brain—contributing critically to CARE, LUST, and PLAY—the SEEKING system facilitates both the enthusiasm for and reinforcement of learning. At the most basic level, this system promotes finding all things in the world needed for survival. Its fundamental nature (prior to learning) is to project children into the world as enthusiastic activists who can look after their own welfare—expertly harvesting both nuts and knowledge, so to speak. This remarkable system, always at the ready most of our waking moments (and super-active also during our dreams that help consolidate life-supporting strategies), is the focus of this book. If we can encourage children to be active seekers of knowledge, many of our educational efforts will have lasting positive consequences for structuring each child's world and future success.

How we do this remains more of an art than a science, but Gregory and Kaufeldt's superb guidelines can enhance success. They provide guidelines for implementing the SEEKING system within our educational practices. The book covers general principles that need to be understood, recommendations for specific practices, and suggestions for implementing these practices. They bring educators a new level of scientific sophistication for discussing the many issues that need to be considered for educational practices to be harmonized with the natural functions of the brain. These are beyond accepted standard-bearers of learning and memory—those who understood the importance of reinforcement contingencies—which had great impact on educational practices during the 20th century.

In 1930, one of the fathers of behaviorism, John Watson, wrote "Give me a dozen healthy infants, well-formed, and my own specified world to bring them up in and I'll guarantee to take any one at random and train him to become any type of specialist I might select—doctor, lawyer, artist, merchant-chief and, yes, even beggar-man and thief, regardless of his talents, penchants, tendencies, abilities, vocations, and race of his ancestors" (Watson, 1930, p. 82). His compatriot, B.F. Skinner, gave us automatic learning machines where rapid reinforcement of correct answers clearly sped up learning. The ingredient that both missed was any discussion of how we help create internally motivated, enthusiastic, active learners. *That* is what a fuller consideration of the SEEKING system in education provides and what this book offers. The book speaks clearly and effectively about how we can recruit the affective emotional-mental resources that all children share to help facilitate the growth of upper-minds with active engagement and with new information and perspectives. Superb teachers implicitly understand such issues, but this book makes many of the issues explicit.

A secondary theme developed by the authors is the benefit that we can achieve by recruiting the powers of PLAY for our educational ends. This primal emotional system that our group first started to study in animal models in the late 1970s has entranced us more than any other, especially as the child-rearing, educational implications became ever clearer for me (Panksepp, Siviy, & Normansell, 1984). This system, which relies heavily on the SEEKING system (as do LUST and CARE), is also subcortically situated in very ancient brain regions. Indeed, our main empirical measure of social joy—"rat laughter" that can be evoked by systematically tickling—maps along the SEEKING system. In every place in the brain where we can evoke such playful sounds with deep brain stimulation, we have found the sites to be rewarding (Burgdorf et al., 2007), which is our main factual evidence for positive feelings in nonspeaking animals.

PLAY arousal appears to be the fundamental source of social joy, which, just like the enthusiasm of the SEEKING system, is at a low ebb in clinical depression (Panksepp et al., 2014). Once we realized that this ancient brain function is elaborated by brain systems below the neocortex, we started to consider how it might affect child-development, especially if young children were deprived of having adequate avenues to express this system each and every day (Panksepp & Scott, 2013). We suspected that deprivation could lead to various Attention Deficit Hyperactivity Disorders (Panksepp 1998). Indeed, to our surprise, all medications typically used to treat ADHD, such as methylphenidate, were strong reducers of play in young animals. Why would psychostimulants reduce psychologically robust behavior such as PLAY? We still don't quite understand the details, but we must be worried about children in the classroom who have not had their fair share of the satisfactions of physical play. Our animal work indicates that abundant play sets in motion many brain systems that not only facilitate learning but promote happiness (Burgdorf et al., 2011). The many benefits of play should alert educators to the problems that may emerge when children are deprived of this vital resource for mental health. Without a regular diet of fun social engagements, children become hungry for play and begin to "act out," potentially disrupting the flow of classroom instructional activities.

We have analyzed higher brain regions for gene-expression patterns, namely the neocortex, following bouts of abundant social play in juvenile animals. Of the approximately 1,200 genes we monitored, one third were significantly jogged one way or another by the playful activities (Burgdorf et al., 2011). Surely this means that playful activities, and other forms of SEEKING, promote a healthier, prosocial learning platform for learning activities and the maturation of happier brains that are resistant to depression (Panksepp et al., 2014).

Indeed, Finland's government has decreed that grade-school children should have 15 minutes of free play during each hour that they are in class. Teachers were initially resistant, but once they saw how effectively this facilitated their teaching efforts, they became staunch supporters of common sense. Indeed, what this fine and uncommon book on educational practices offers is a vision of how we can maximize the vast potential benefits of education, by getting better acquainted with the intrinsic emotional/motivational powers of children's minds. Through an appreciation of these universal 'lower' powers of their minds, we may have more success in molding the 'higher' spaces into receptacles for all the intellectual riches that we have to offer.

In sum, it is becoming increasingly clear that the higher intellectual qualities of human minds, just as those of other animals, are constructed by diverse emotional and motivational circuits in the brain that mediate diverse feelings that are currently illuminating, for the first time, how affective experiences are created within all mammalian brains. Better ways to utilize such mental energies to facilitate class-room activities are superbly summarized in this remarkable book.

Jaak Panksepp
Professor of Neuroscience and Baily Endowed
    Chair for Animal Well-Being Science
Department of Integrative Physiology and Neuroscience
Washington State University
Pullman, WA

Introduction

Motivation, enthusiasm, perseverance, drive, grit, and tenacity are currently very hot topics in education. Understanding how to get students to pay attention and engage in rigorous tasks is something *every* teacher desires.

The field of cognitive psychology provides educators with many models about how to trigger motivation and keep students engaged. For example, Stanford psychologist Carol Dweck's (2006) work helps teachers understand how to promote growth mindsets versus fixed mindsets. In 2013, the U.S. Department of Education published a report titled *Promoting Grit, Tenacity, and Perseverance: Critical Factors for Success in the 21st Century* (Shechtman et al., 2013) that noted that beyond content knowledge, it is imperative for educators to learn how to address a core set of noncognitive skills. "These factors are essential to an individual's capacity to strive for and succeed at long-term and higher-order goals, and to persist in the face of the array of challenges and obstacles encountered throughout schooling and life" (p. 19). The document makes strong recommendations about how the educational community must shift priorities and begin to design learning environments that promote the attributes, dispositions, social skills, and attitudes of these critical noncognitive skills.

In addition, the new scientific discipline of affective neuroscience takes into consideration basic mental processes, brain functions, and emotional behaviors that all mammals share. It combines the study of the neural mechanisms of emotions as well as the psychological study of mood, feelings, and personality. By studying mammal brains and using neuroimaging technologies, Jaak Panksepp, Kent Berridge, and other neuroscientists have been able to locate and identify the ancient neural networks where primal emotions are generated (see, e.g., Panksepp & Biven, 2012; Pecina & Berridge, 2013). These ancient neural systems are located in the subcortical area of the human brain, deep below the neocortex—our "thinking cap." We can now identify the specific locations in the brain where motivation and enthusiasm are generated. Investigating these emotions will help psychiatrists and mental health professionals design more effective treatments. But educators and parents, too, will benefit, by discovering insights into child development, behavior, and how these primary emotions shape our feelings, mold our motivations, and ultimately influence learning.

Educators have a keen interest in understanding how they might improve student attention, perseverance, and engagement. This book will link the cognitive psychology models with affective neuroscience and provide practical examples of how educators can promote enthusiasm, generate motivation, and encourage perseverance in even the most disengaged student.

Our Background

For almost four decades, we have investigated emerging research in cognitive psychology and educational neuroscience and have attempted to translate the findings into practical classroom applications. We have written many books for educators on how instruction and student success might be improved if the strategies that teachers used were compatible with what we know about how brains learn naturally. Originally referred to as "brain-based" and "brain-compatible" teaching, this instructional pedagogy is now often labeled "brain-friendly." The philosophy and strategies encompass the following elements:

- The design of the learning *environment*
- The use and scheduling of *time*

- The integration of *play* and *joyfulness*
- Opportunities for *firsthand learning* and *outdoor experiences*
- The importance of *collaboration* and *social interactions*
- Relevant and *meaningful connections* to the content
- Respectful understanding of students' cultures, interests, and prior experiences
- The importance of student voice, choice, and self-determination

In the last few years, our work—including this book—has been dramatically influenced by the research of Dr. Jaak Panksepp from Washington State University. In 2012, at the Learning and the Brain conference in San Francisco, Panksepp presented his theory that many children today never get sufficient amounts of natural, self-generated play. He concludes that this may be one of the reasons that children develop hyperactivity and attention disorders and also lack impulse control. Panksepp's research has led him to help launch an emerging scientific discipline referred to as *affective neuroscience*. This branch of brain research is the study of the neural mechanisms of basic animal and human emotions. This interdisciplinary field combines neuroscience with the psychological study of personality, emotion, and mood.

Panksepp has spent his career first identifying and then studying seven primary emotional processes that are shared by all mammals. He contends that SEEKING is an inherited primary emotional process and is the key to survival, learning, and connections. This amazing research contributes to our understanding of the neuroscience of motivation and the SEEKING system that we discuss in this book. Understanding this basic primary emotion will help us understand motivation. The research around SEEKING, and especially its role in the release of dopamine, confirms many of the points that educational innovators have been suggesting:

- The effects of chronic stress and poverty have a great influence on a student's chance to be motivated and to ultimately succeed.
- Opportunities to play and socialize within a safe and secure climate and environment promote a student's motivation.

- A growth mindset and the ability to persevere when faced with setbacks are skills that can be developed with practice and opportunities to make mistakes.
- Relevant real-world projects and problems that demand imagination, creativity, problem solving, and communication skills (i.e., 21st century skills) can be highly motivating to students at any age.
- Opportunities to play, create, and work with peers are successful instructional strategies and motivators at any grade level, and they shouldn't be dismissed in secondary and higher education settings.
- Integrating the routine use of age-appropriate current technology is imperative to inspire student motivation.

Outdated Educational Systems

Many of us are concerned that students in our classrooms today will not be prepared to adapt, create, persevere, innovate, and solve problems as they become adults. With technology advancements happening at astonishing rates, the gap between what students know and what they need to know to be successful after graduation is widening quickly. According to educator Alfie Kohn (2014a):

> Traditional schooling isn't working for an awful lot of students. We can respond to that fact either by trying to fix the system (so it meets kids' needs better) or by trying to fix the kids (so they're more compliant and successful at whatever they're told to do).

It often seems that the very champions claiming to be most invested in education are responsible for the paralysis of our fundamental beliefs about education and our elaborate, though archaic, delivery systems. In *Human Brain and Human Learning* (1983), Leslie Hart posited that designing educational experiences without knowledge about how human brains learn naturally and most efficiently can be compared to designing a glove without any knowledge of the human hand. More than 30 years later, how can our educational system continue to promote and implement curriculum and programs that don't seem to "fit" with how brains learn? How can we then complain about a poor educational system, unmotivated students, and less than stellar assessment results?

We know that young human brains are intrinsically motivated. They are enthusiastically SEEKING, in Panksepp's term, in an ongoing and positive way. Shouldn't classrooms be designed and orchestrated to maximize opportunities to explore and engage with the concepts and skills most appropriate for success in the 21st century?

Try It, You'll Like It

Pritchard and Ashwood (2008) define motivation as "the process used to allocate energy to maximize the satisfaction of needs" (p. 6). Our challenge as educators is this: how can we encourage students to allocate some of their energy into their learning and school experiences? If we examine how intrinsic motivation is generated in the brain, might we be able to understand ways to design classroom environments and curriculum experiences to encourage students to demonstrate more motivation to learn? Neuroscience research is suggesting that intrinsically motivated behaviors are actually *exploratory* behaviors. By investigating recent research in the field of affective neuroscience, we can gain a better understanding of the elusive "motivation X factor."

For teachers who may feel like they don't have autonomy or the flexibility to implement strategies to promote student motivation, we say, "Just do it"! Even if these strategies are implemented sporadically and interspersed within traditional one-size-fits-all instructional strategies, students will appreciate the opportunities to think, collaborate, and create. Even infrequent implementation may encourage unmotivated students.

We have found research on the SEEKING system to be a great help to us as we rethink curriculum design and classroom instruction in an effort to promote student engagement and motivation. We believe that the information and strategies you'll find in this book will inspire you to continue SEEKING powerful learning opportunities for your own students.

Part I

Understanding Motivation

1

The Challenge of Motivating Students

Engagement and motivation—what's the difference? Teachers everywhere strive to motivate their students and engage them in learning. Can we really motivate others, or is it a personal thing that happens when conditions are right? The English words *motivation* and *movement* are derived from the Latin *movere*, "to move." The German philosopher Schopenhauer (1999) suggested that motivation was the result of all organisms being in a position to "choose, seize and even seek out satisfaction." Neo-behaviorists Hull and Spence used terms such as *drive* and *incentive* as synonyms for motivational concepts.

Paul Thomas Young (1961) defined motivation as the process of generating actions, sustaining them, and regulating the activity.

Salamone (2010) suggests that motivation processes allow organisms to regulate their internal and external environment, seeking access to some stimuli and avoiding others. Sutherland and Oswald (2005) suggest that engagement is not just a simple reaction of a student to a teacher's action but is much more complex.

Although there are many definitions of motivation, with some stressing the notion of movement that would suggest engagement, we should not assume that motivation and engagement are synonymous. Sometimes the terms are used interchangeably, but really *motivation is the force or energy that results in engagement.* In a classroom, the complex interaction of teacher, student, and curriculum helps to create motivation that yields high engagement.

Motivation, Drive, Tenacity, and Grit

Motivation, drive, tenacity, and grit are currently hot topics. A variety of opinions and theories are emerging from cognitive psychology about how important these skills are to one's success in life and how to promote them.

Self-Efficacy

Students arrive at school with an already well-developed self-image of competence or incompetence resulting from messages they have received at home since birth. Whether they have been encouraged to persevere when faced with challenges or coddled and discouraged from taking risks to overcome obstacles, students' beliefs about their abilities will affect their level of motivation and engagement. A learner's self-efficacy (one's belief in one's ability to succeed in specific situations) can greatly influence his or her motivation. In general, students with high self-efficacy are more likely to give more effort to complete a task and to persist longer than a student with low self-efficacy (Bandura, 1986). Their world-view of "never give up" and can-do attitude are essential to success.

Social beliefs related to gender or race also contribute to one's mindset about performance level. Gender bias messages or cultural cues may influence whether students feel capable or possibly doomed to failure (Aronson & Steele, 2005). These beliefs can be instrumental in helping to motivate discouraged learners.

The Yerkes-Dodson Law of Arousal

Each of us reacts to a stimulus differently. For example, a project or task offered to a group of students will prompt a full range of responses related to motivation, from excitement to boredom. Students will react negatively or positively depending on how they perceive the difficulty of the task or the challenge involved and the interests they have. Their mindsets as to the probability of success will influence their excitement or frustration facing the task and thus, ultimately, their motivation.

The relationship between pressure (arousal) and one's performance is known as the Yerkes-Dodson law (Yerkes & Dodson, 2007). See Figure 1.1. As stress and pressure rise, performance usually improves. At the peak of the curve, one has reached "maximum cognitive efficiency" (Damasio, 2003). One's performance will not likely improve no matter how much additional pressure or stress is exerted. In fact, performance and motivation may begin to diminish if pressure continues. We can benefit from the endorphin rush that occurs when we increase our level of stimulation by pushing ourselves physically or mentally, but the apex of optimal performance is a tipping point. Like the Goldilocks theory, the Yerkes-Dodson law notes that in some cases there could be either too low or too intense an arousal. The ratio of stress to performance needs to be "just right" for each individual learner in order to maintain motivation.

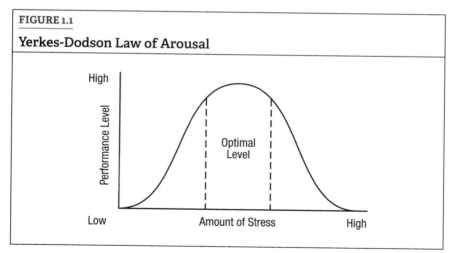

FIGURE 1.1

Yerkes-Dodson Law of Arousal

We need to strive to provide the "just right" balance of excitement and challenge without undue stress for our students. Prior experience with similar tasks may influence one's reaction and degree of motivation. Tiered lessons and adjustable assignments (Gregory & Chapman, 2013) attempt to do this. So the trick is to find the optimum level of challenge that engages, and is enjoyable and safe for every learner (see the sections on flow and the zone of proximal development in Chapter 6).

Drive

In *Drive: The Surprising Truth About What Motivates Us*, Daniel Pink discusses research from the last 50 years on *intrinsic motivation*—motivation that comes from within ourselves. Carrot-and-stick enticements, or *extrinsic rewards*, not only don't work in the long run but may actually lower performance, stifle creativity, and decrease the desired behavior. We have an inherent tendency to seek out novelty and challenges, to extend and build our capacities, to explore, and to learn (Pink, 2009). Mostly people are motivated to do interesting work with supportive colleagues.

In his research, Pink found that people do not respond to monetary rewards and punishments as compared with being given the opportunity for
- autonomy—people want to have control over their work;
- mastery—people want to get better at what they do; and
- purpose—people want to be part of something that is bigger than they are.

Grit

Another popular look at motivation includes research gathered by Angela Duckworth, a psychology professor at the University of Pennsylvania. She suggests that grit entails "working strenuously toward challenges, maintaining effort and interest over years despite failure, adversity and plateaus in progress" (Duckworth, Peterson, Matthews, & Kelly, 2007, p. 1087). Duckworth and her colleagues define grit as "perseverance and passion for long-term goals," (p. 1087). Grit can be a positive indicator of success in the long haul. It adds the component of passion to the trait of persistence. The Intelligence Quotient (IQ) is not always the determining factor in student success, but grit can be, although it is not tied to intelligence. We need to rethink how hard and where we challenge students with unfamiliar and uncomfortable tasks. Many students with a high intelligence may decide to take the safe route and are not particularly successful in life, whereas students with average intelligence and a good level of grit often far surpass their high-ability peers as grit predicts success beyond talent.

Grit is not just having resilience to overcome adversity, bounce back from challenges, or survive at-risk environments. Grit is also staying the course, much like the Tortoise in the famed fable. The Tortoise persists even though his journey is slower and more tedious. The Tortoise wins the race because the Hare (a more talented runner) meanders and becomes distracted along the way. Grit is about being able to commit over time and remain loyal to goals that are set (Duckworth et al., 2007). Developing grit requires multiple rehearsals with content or skills to achieve success and develop mastery. We teachers must tap our creativity to provide the practice that diverse learners need, making sure to offer a variety of multisensory tasks that appeal to students' varied learning preferences. This practice blends the "art of teaching" based on what we know from the research base of impactful strategies, and the "science" of teaching (Hattie, 2009; Marzano, Pickering, & Pollock, 2001).

We must be careful not to come at grit from a fear-based focus on testing and college selection, especially with young adolescent brains that are more susceptible to negative or critical reactions. Poorly informed teachers and parents may attribute a lack of success to a lack of grit without analyzing the full situation with regard to other issues, such as missing support or resources. Psychologists refer to this sort of misperception as "fundamental attribution error." In addition, perseverance that emphasizes punishments and rewards will undermine long-term grit. Grit is different from passion because grit requires effort and fully engaged commitment to be successful.

The Secret to Success Is Failure

In *How Children Succeed: Grit, Curiosity and the Hidden Power of Character*, Paul Tough (2012) makes significant contributions to Duckworth's notion of grit in regard to education. He postulates that in the real world, learning to react to failure is as critical to success as academic achievement. Noncognitive character traits such as resilience, persistence, drive, and delayed gratification are as important as cognitive skills (Farrington et al., 2012). If we don't learn how to deal with frustration and obstacles, we are not likely to choose challenging or risky paths and will perhaps lead a life of mediocrity and predictability. The trait of delaying gratification is necessary to persevere despite encountering obstacles.

Emotional Intelligence

Emotional intelligence (EI) is a person's ability to use her or his emotions mindfully. It consists of a balance between emotions and reasoning. Daniel Goleman (1995) believes that EI, like grit, is more important than IQ.

Goleman describes EI as composed of five emotional competencies, or domains: self-awareness, managing emotions, self-motivation, empathy, and social skills. He regards these domains as the keys to success in the 21st century.

• **Self-awareness.** This domain entails our ability to identify and name our feelings and to articulate our emotions. We can differentiate with precision a feeling and identify (beyond a basic feeling such as sadness) the more complex feelings of anxiety, upset, depression, or disappointment. We are not engulfed with the feelings and can name and then deal with them.

• **Managing emotions.** Once feelings are labeled, we can begin to think about how to handle them—how to soothe or change the mood or, if anger is the issue, how to resolve conflict.

• **Self-motivation.** If we can motivate ourselves, we can develop competencies such as setting goals, delaying gratification, and persisting. Being able to self-motivate is actually a state of mind—a certain level of mindfulness. Those who are self-motivated are often more successful in life, unrelated to their socioeconomic position and cognitive intelligence, because they have an inner drive and determination to persist.

• **Empathy.** Empathy is the ability to feel for someone else or to stand in another's shoes. Being able to read and understand the feelings of another builds tolerance.

• **Social skills.** People with good social skills have the ability to use interpersonal skills to interact appropriately with others. They are able to read and respond to people in a positive way. They are said to have "social polish." Their teamwork skills are refined, they are collaborative, and they have social influence.

Emotional intelligence derives from the communication between your emotional and rational "brains." Initially, primary senses enter the spinal cord and move through the limbic system (emotional center) to the frontal lobe of your brain before you can think rationally about your experience. In other words, an emotional reaction occurs before our rational mind is activated. Emotional intelligence requires a balance between the rational and emotional centers of the brain (see Figure 1.2).

FIGURE 1.2

Emotional Intelligence

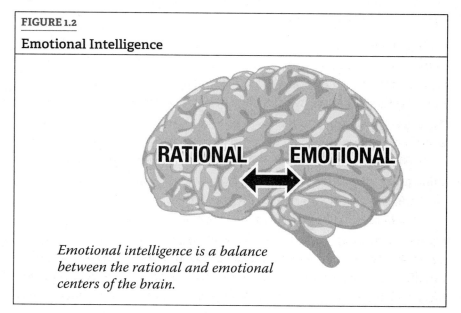

Emotional intelligence is a balance between the rational and emotional centers of the brain.

Plasticity is the term neuroscientists use to describe the brain's ability to grow and change. The change is incremental, but as we consciously practice new skills, permanent habits form. Using strategies to increase emotional intelligence allows the creation of billions of neural connections (dendritic growth) between the rational and emotional areas of the brain. A single cell can grow up to 15,000 connections (dendrites) with nearby neurons. We make new connections as we learn new skills, including emotional intelligence strategies. Practicing will strengthen those neural connections, and over time new behaviors will become habits.

Figure 1.3 lists the five domains of emotional intelligence and suggestions to foster this trait in students, with possible applications that may support the domain.

FIGURE 1.3

How to Foster Emotional Intelligence

Domains	How to Foster	Application
Self-awareness Ability to identify and name a feeling or emotion and how it might affect others.	Have discussions to help students differentiate emotions and label them.	Write in journals or logs. Share reflections.
Managing emotions Labeling feelings and responding accordingly; includes self-regulation.	Help students identify feelings and discuss how they might best respond. Use "teachable moments" when situations happen.	Take a deep breath. Count to 10. Take a walk. Do something else. Create distractions.
Self-motivation Ability to set goals, persist, and delay gratification.	Help students develop strategies to persist and problem solve to continue to move forward.	Set goals. Brainstorm how to persist. Problem solve.
Empathy Ability to feel for another and understand his or her feelings.	Prompt students to think about others' feelings and feel "with them."	Model empathy. Discuss issues where feelings for others are identified and reflected on.
Social skills Ability to "read" another person, respond appropriately, and build rapport and common ground.	Explicitly teach social skills. Practice social skills when using group work.	Model skills. Suggest appropriate language.

Source: Adapted from Bradberry and Greaves (2009). This resource provides concrete, practical ways to increase one's emotional intelligence.

Belief Through Effort

Fredricks (2014) suggests a view of engagement that considers behavioral, emotional, and cognitive engagement and their integration.

Behavioral engagement consists of such things as positive actions (e.g., compliance with classroom rules and school norms), nondisruptive behaviors (attendance and orderliness), effort and participation, and school community involvement (sports and clubs). Students who have behavioral engagement "play the school game" and it is easy to observe these students. Engagement here refers mainly to on-task behavior.

Emotional engagement entails students' emotional reactions to school, whether there is a feeling of belonging, and whether they value tasks and school. Emotionally engaged students are vested in school and connected to it. This type of engagement is often overlooked. The more interest, positive attitude, and task satisfaction (without anxiety, stress, and boredom), the greater the engagement.

Cognitive engagement refers to students' investment in tasks and challenges, as well as their perseverance in completing and tackling challenges. They are aware of what they are doing and why, both hands-on and "minds-on" for a specific strategy or task. Cognitive engagement also includes self-regulation, strategic planning, and reflection. It often is described as "deep" rather than "surface" learning.

Self-Determination Theory

Self-determination theory (SDT) suggests that we are driven by a desire to continually grow and reach fulfillment (Deci & Ryan, 1985). We are centrally concerned with how to move ourselves or others to act. We need to master challenges and experiences to develop our sense of self. Deci and Ryan recognize two basic reward systems, intrinsic and extrinsic. Intrinsic rewards tap into inner potential and interests, allowing us to express our true self and growth. Extrinsic rewards provide tangible rewards or incentives such as stickers, pizza parties, and bonuses. Deci and Ryan suggest that individuals tend to move toward the innate need to grow and gain fulfillment. We need to feel the following to satisfy and achieve psychological growth:

- Competence and mastery of skills
- Connections and relatedness and a sense of belonging
- Autonomy, or a sense of control over their goals and behavior

If we achieve these, we become self-determined and are intrinsically motivated to pursue what is meaningful to us. Being constantly tempted and enticed by rewards undermines the intrinsic motivation that already exists in each of us. *Motivational crowding out* is the term used to describe how external rewards (e.g., money, prizes, recognition) may crowd out intrinsic rewards of a job well done and enjoyed. Thus, the common classroom practice of rewarding students with stickers, privileges, and so forth, can backfire when it comes to long-term motivation.

Deci, Koestner, and Ryan (1999) also suggests that intermittent positive encouragement and feedback on performance can increase one's intrinsic motivation. Positive feedback makes us feel more competent and enhances personal growth. Deci and Ryan explain that the social environment has an impact on the growth. The environment can enhance or disrupt the growth of the human psyche. "Social environments can, according to this perspective, either facilitate and enable the growth and integration propensities with which the human psyche is endowed, or they can disrupt, forestall, and fragment these processes resulting in behaviors and inner experiences that represent the darker side of humanity" (Deci & Ryan, 1985, p. 6).

Punished by Rewards

Alfie Kohn (1999) talks about "punishment by reward" wherein we lose a sense of joy and accomplishment (i.e., intrinsic reward) because we are coerced into action by extrinsic rewards rather than spurred on by innate motivation. Kohn cautions that extrinsic rewards—"carrots"—may work in the short run but not in the long run; in fact, manipulating people with incentives may actually cause harm. He suggests these rewards only result in temporary obedience and do nothing to increase drive because most people lose interest in tasks that they are doing only for the reward. Rewards turn what should be satisfying tasks into drudgery. Often lower-quality work is the outcome. Kohn cites 70 studies showing that the incentives/rewards such as As and pizza parties are not effective and can be counterproductive in the long term in regard to instilling a desire to learn and a strong work ethic in students. Praise is also not helpful, because it supports the idea of "fixed mindset" or intelligence (Dweck, 2006). More effective is corrective and supportive timely feedback and the encouragement for effort.

What if we got rid of grades and praise and focused on real learning? If the behavior needs to be manipulated to achieve compliance, perhaps something is wrong with the task. If learning is interesting, challenging, and meaningful, doing the work is its own reward. Students should not have to be coerced or manipulated to complete it.

Basic Needs and Choice Theory

The brain's original purpose was not to go to school but to survive and thrive. Several theorists have suggested which basic needs are most important to humans and suggest that these needs must be met in order to allow us to eventually focus on learning.

In 1968, psychologist Abraham Maslow proposed a hierarchy of human needs beginning with the most basic, as listed here (see also Figure 1.4). These needs must be met before we can move to self-actualization.

- Physiological needs: food, water, air, shelter
- Safety needs: security, order, freedom from fear
- Belongingness and love: friends, spouse, children, family
- Self-esteem: self-respect, achievement, reputation
- Self-actualization: becoming what the individual has the potential to become

Glasser's (1990, 1998) choice theory of motivation cites five important needs. These are similar to Maslow's needs in many ways, although they are not arranged hierarchically (see Figure 1.5). Glasser suggests that all we do is behave, and almost all behavior is chosen. His choice theory focuses on the growth of relationships and not external control.

FIGURE 1.4

Maslow's Hierarchy of Needs

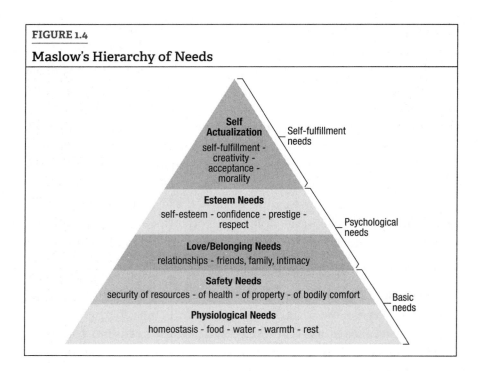

The behaviors that we choose are a personal choice and are always within our own control. Glasser suggests that we are driven by genes and have the following needs:

- The need to survive and procreate
- The need to belong and love
- The need to have some power
- The need for freedom
- The need to have fun

Glasser believes the need to belong, which parallels Maslow's need for belongingness, is most important. If students feel disconnected and frustrated that their needs are not met, they will likely give up. A sense of not belonging is a major source of school failure (Glasser, 1998). Students need to feel that they belong and have some choices and a certain degree of personal control.

FIGURE 1.5

Glasser's Basic Needs

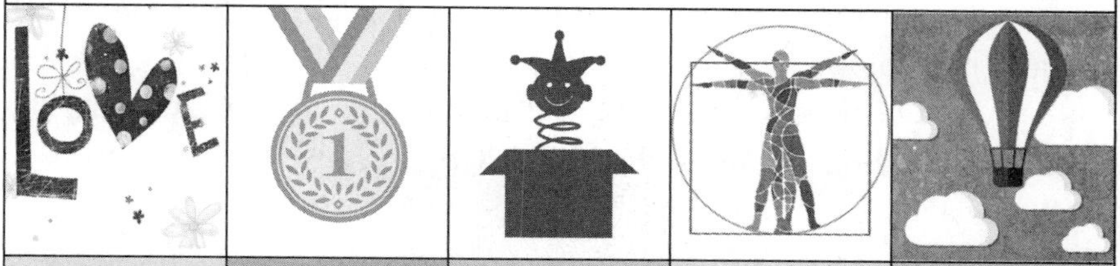

Love & Belonging	Power	Fun	Survival	Freedom
• belonging • being loved • being respected • friendship • sharing • cooperation	• recognition • success • importance • achievement • skills	• enjoyment • laughter • learning • change	• health • relaxation • sexual activity • food • warmth	• choices • independence • freedom from • freedom to

Choice theory focuses on seven caring habits that create conditions that draw people together and, conversely, seven deadly habits that push people apart and strain relationships.

Seven Caring Habits	Seven Deadly Habits
Supporting	Criticizing
Encouraging	Blaming
Listening	Complaining
Accepting	Nagging
Trusting	Threatening
Respecting	Punishing
Negotiating differences	Rewarding/Bribing to control

Choice theory also revolves around the following beliefs:

1. We can only control our behavior.
2. Information is all we can give someone else.
3. Most psychological problems are relationship problems.

4. Our past has everything to do with what we do today, but only our basic needs can be satisfied right now.

5. All behavior is made up of four elements: acting, thinking, feeling, and physiology.

6. We have direct control over acting and thinking, but we only control our feeling and physiology indirectly by how we choose to think and act.

Both Maslow's and Glasser's theories stress the notion of basic needs taking precedent over all else. As we think about motivating our students, we must recognize that their basic needs—as well as other needs such as feeling safe and belonging—must be met before they can focus on fulfilling higher-order needs such as learning and self-development.

Self-Efficacy

Another theory with implications for motivation is Bandura's (1986, 1997) theory of self-efficacy. His basic premise is that people will engage in activities if they believe that they are competent in them. Students will be more likely to engage, persist, and succeed at tasks when they feel a sense of efficacy. Failure may be due to a lack of skills or the efficacy to use them. Bandura identifies the following classroom practices that inhibit feelings of positive self-efficacy:

- Direct instruction where students can get lost in the progression
- Low-ability groupings
- Highly competitive practices where some learners can't possibly succeed

In contrast, Schunk (1989) suggests the following strategies to enhance students' self-efficacy:

- Setting attainable personal goals
- Modeling statements of self-efficacy
- Focusing on constructive feedback
- Encouraging learners to articulate and share strategies that work

Diminished Student Engagement and Motivation: Eight Possible Reasons

What is responsible for lack of motivation? Educators across the country, teaching all socioeconomic groups, are asking, "Why aren't these kids motivated?" As indicated by the theories just discussed, many factors can contribute to students' lack of motivation. Other possible reasons include the infusion of technology into students' lives, the expectation of immediate gratification, chronic stress, and living in impoverished conditions. These issues may not be in our locus of control.

But there are several school factors that we believe are contributing to low student motivation. These include lack of real-world application, apathy from students deriving from instructional mediocrity, social isolation (and bullying), and fixed mindsets. Fortunately, these are all aspects of education that we *can* do something about.

Technology

The digital natives coming to school today are very adept with and used to using technology that they are not allowed to experience in most classrooms. We sometimes have a skewed viewpoint when it comes to technology, blaming the distractibility of technology for students' lack of engagement and learning.

Indeed, if we do nothing more than replace textbooks and encyclopedias with Google or Bing, or use the computer or tablet for nothing but writing exercises, technology in the classroom is not as motivating as using these tools to SEEK, find, and use information for problem solving and creativity. Advanced engagement through higher-order thinking and production are preferable uses for technology over the pursuit of trivia or gaming.

Unfortunately, because of a lack of hardware and sometimes teacher confidence and creativity, students are denied access to the very strongest engagement resource we have—technology. As we discuss in the next chapter, dopamine releases when students have a chance to seek and explore using technology. Whether for research, inquiry, problem-based learning, remediation, or enrichment, many educators are missing the boat in terms of using technology to intrigue and engage learners.

Immediate Gratification

Some blame students' apathy or lack of engagement on the fact that learners today are a "now" generation: if they don't succeed on the first try, they give up. This learned behavior evolves from lack of persistence. When a student has had a series of failures or depends on others to help, that student may develop learned helplessness. Persistence can be frustrating as one struggles with issues or problems, which increases stress and the release of cortisol rather than dopamine, which in turn diminishes the commitment to a task. The cycle becomes one of "I try, I don't succeed; I feel bad, so I give up."

Apathy

Some students come to school at age 5 full of enthusiasm and excitement. For them, kindergarten and the elementary years introduce enough novelty, interesting tasks, and challenges to hold their attention. For other students, however, and in less inspiring classrooms, apathy can creep in. Direct instruction with little student interaction or project work, and problem solving under the guise of "covering the curriculum" to succeed on standardized tests are classroom practices that can foster apathy among our students. Some students "play the school game" and endure the monotony of day-to-day rote learning and lecture models, regarding education as their "job" and a means to an end (e.g., graduating, attending college, or finding a job). A large population of students can become bored and disengaged as the lessons are repetitive, lack relevance to their real world, and require only low-level thinking skills. Their passive receptivity to learning with a lack of emotional and cognitive engagement is perceived as apathy, when actually instructional mediocrity is at the root of the problem.

Lack of Relevance to the Real World

Many students believe that some of what is taught in school has no real meaning in the real world. Being told that this is "good to know" or "You might need this someday" is not necessarily engaging if you are only interested in the here and now. As educators, we need to be more overt and transparent as we connect student assignments to curriculum standards as well as real-world standards. Helping students see how writing a report, delivering opinions supported by evidence, and learning to collaborate, for example, are useful abilities in *any* professional role as well as in their personal life will let students see the curriculum's applicability to their lives. Offering students choices of problems and issues to address in math, science, and social studies that affect or will affect their world in the future can be more motivating than traditional textbook work.

Fixed Mindsets About One's Ability

Carol Dweck (2006) notes that some people develop a fixed notion of their intelligence, whereas others have a growth mindset. With a fixed mindset, we believe that we are born with a certain limited potential that blocks expansive thinking and fosters a lack of drive. On the other hand, a growth mindset involves the belief that with effort and persistence, we will improve, master tasks, and succeed. If students have come to believe in a fixed mindset, they feel there is no use trying. If they have endured seven or eight years of this approach, they can become passive, discouraged students who are not optimistic about the future and disengage so as not to fail.

Brooks and Goldstein (2008) say more effective teachers have a growth mindset that guides their behavior in the classroom. They convey a belief in the potential of all students through their words and modeling so that students in turn develop a growth mindset and become more willing to persevere despite setbacks.

Poverty

Depending on where you live there may be at least 20 percent of children who live in poverty. Based on 2010 census data:

- 22 percent of American children live in poverty
- 39 percent of black children live in poverty
- 35 percent of Hispanic children live in poverty

Children who have grown up in poverty have different brains for a variety of reasons: they may be malnourished resulting from a poor diet; they may have had fewer academic experiences and opportunities and so have limited prior knowledge in some subjects; their vocabulary, verbal skills, and language patterns may be limited. If they are second language learners and live in poverty, they have a double issue. They may perceive their social status as "less than" some peers, and their self-esteem may be low. Research shows that their IQ may be 30 to 40 percent lower than their peers (Griggs & Walker, 2008).

Social Isolation

Many students—not just those in poverty—do not feel comfortable in school. They don't find it a safe haven for body or mind, and thus their basic needs are not being met. They are isolated for many reasons. Students who are English language learners perhaps lack motivation to engage in conversation or just can't make sense of new concepts and therefore may develop learned helplessness. They may be illegal aliens or members of a migrant family who know that they are not going to be in their location for long and thus don't want to become attached to or involved in the school culture. For other students, sexual orientation may be an issue that prevents them from becoming engaged with others or with the academic content. Some students with different cultural backgrounds have a difficult time connecting to what is being taught and how it relates to their prior knowledge or skills. There is often little effort made by the teacher to connect to their culture and make a "bridge" for the learning. A high degree of racism or bullying may be present in school that emotionally hijacks students. They are too occupied with self-preservation (physical or psychological) to be concerned with learning. All these conditions mean that students' basic needs are not being met, and thus paying attention to what we think is important is not high on their list of priorities (National Research Council, 2003). These conditions also can create stress, the topic of the next section.

Students Under Stress and Perceived Threat

Stress, excessive pressure, and perceived threat can temporarily shut down enthusiastic motivation as our brains go into a default reflex response.

The brain contains a sensory screening process—basically a survival mechanism—whereby the brain scans the horizon for a potential threat. On the savannah, a threat might have been a wild predator. In modern classrooms, a variety of situations and circumstances may be perceived as threats and cause undue anxiety and stress: fear of ridicule or punishment, exclusion, being asked to keep seated and quiet, isolation from classmates, unclear expectations, or tasks that are too easy or too difficult.

The brain's survival mechanism to respond to perceived threats in the environment is the reticular activating system (RAS), a primitive network of cells in the lower brainstem that acts as the gatekeeper to what information flows into parts of the brain responsible for higher-order tasks, such as learning. Under normal conditions, the amygdala directs incoming data to the prefrontal cortex (PFC), where the information can be sent processed into long-term memory.

The amygdala, located deep in the temporal lobes, triggers the body and brain to react with the appropriate fight, flight, or freeze response to the crisis and releases of a high level of stress hormones. This *reflexive* response takes over, and the executive, *reflective* brain functions are temporarily bypassed. When there is unmanageable stress, self-preservation takes over, motivation is reduced, and learning is minimized.

Neuroimaging has provided information about which parts of the brain are engaged when a threat is present. Emotions such as fear, anger, or sadness interfere with learning as the activity in the brain remains in primitive areas instead of in the PFC. The RAS sends the sensory input to the lower areas of the brain. The brain does its original job in protecting the person from harm. The RAS directs the threatening sensory input through the amygdala to the primitive brain where fight, flight, or freeze is the order of the day. The primitive brain is in control, and the real sensory input students need for learning isn't directed to the PFC (Raz & Buhle, 2006). If this stress persists, the amygdala is under constant stress and information is blocked from the PFC, as the brain can only focus on survival rather than the content or skills being taught. It's not that students are not paying attention. They are—but not necessarily to the things we want them to. The response to stress also may produce inappropriate behavioral responses when the brain is in the fight, flight, or freeze survival mode, with students often zoning out or acting out. Their reduced academic success affects their self-confidence and reinforces a fixed mindset and often learned helplessness.

Rather than threat, it is important that novelty, interesting ideas, and curiosity-arousing items—including music and colors—are present in the classroom to stimulate the RAS. Then the "door" to the PFC is open (Wang et al., 2005). Instructional elements like these can be particularly motivating and attention grabbing, allowing students to relax and enjoy learning with very low threat. This environment increases the possibility of "velcroing" information or concepts to the mind and transferring learning into long-term memory.

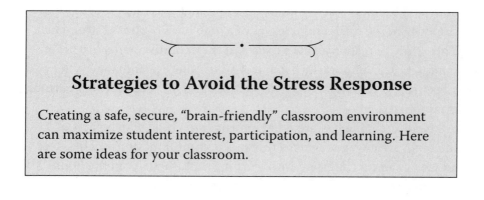

Strategies to Avoid the Stress Response

Creating a safe, secure, "brain-friendly" classroom environment can maximize student interest, participation, and learning. Here are some ideas for your classroom.

Classroom Norms

Students can often experience "anticipatory anxiety" when they are unsure of the conditions, processes, and expectations for success. Predictable, consistent, and shared procedures for arriving at and starting class, distributing materials, and accomplishing daily routines lower stress and provide a comfortable environment. If we can set up routines and procedures so that the brain does not have to resort to the fight, flight, or freeze response, we will alleviate a lot of stress and distraction. The brain looks for patterns and can use them to move about the room and manage materials, resources, and interactions.

Classroom norms or behaviors related to how the teacher and students work together in the classroom also create a safety net and reduce potential conflict as students work collaboratively. Behavior guidelines for how students work alone, in a group, or as a class will greater ensure a stable environment and contribute to organization and orderliness. Establish procedures for these activities:

- What students do when they come into class
- Who gives out materials
- How and where students hand in assignments
- What to do when students finish their work
- What students can do when they don't know what to do
- What to do when students need help
- Procedures for how to get into groups
- How students work with others
- How students tidy the classroom and dismissal procedures

These practices all help to free the self-preservation mode in students' brains, allowing them to engage fully in pursuit of learning. Classroom norms need to be negotiated if students have ideas or suggestions and should be posted so students can use them as a resource to help develop independence and self-efficacy. The routines need to be demonstrated, practiced, and monitored so that students know them well. These procedures become automatic over time as the brain connections are strengthened through repetition.

Group Work

Hallowell (2011) suggests that people need to interact with others daily to satisfy our human biological needs and that evidence indicates that people deprived of this interaction will actually *lose* brain cells. It is essential that classrooms are true learning communities where everyone has a sense of belonging and feels included. Teachers must foster that community spirit by facilitating collaboration with partners and in small groups focused on rigorous, interesting, appropriately challenging academic tasks with opportunities for developing social skills. There is much more "brain safety" in a small group to share and build on one another's ideas, admit confusion, and make mistakes than to risk embarrassment in a large group or as a lone voice (Gregory & Kaufeldt, 2012).

Agendas

Agendas for the day or period will also give the brain the foreshadowing it needs to be ready for upcoming activities and tasks that students will encounter. Agendas elicit curiosity and facilitate smooth transitions. Students should also be clear about the goals or standards that are being targeted in the lesson(s) or unit, the tasks expected of them, and the criteria for success (e.g., rubrics), so that they can self-regulate and monitor their learning. Stress is also reduced when students are able to be self-directed and have choices in tasks and "how they show what they know." The time and encouragement to reflect on personal progress and set goals also gives students a sense of control and autonomy.

Movement

Movement is necessary in the classroom. When we sit, blood "pools" and does not flow to the brain where it is needed. The brain needs 20 percent of the body's glucose and oxygen, says Daniel Drubach (2000). Moving helps reoxygenate the blood and pump it to the brain. This biological process in itself is a wake-up call. Movement releases feel-good hormones, endorphins, and dopamine; it also lowers the levels of the stress hormones (cortisol and adrenaline). The combined effect reduces stress and helps give a sense of well-being and comfort.

Create reasons for movement by asking students to form a group, move their desks and chairs to work together, or engage in a standing partner dialogue. In the elementary grades, play "Simon Says" or sing a movement song. Brain Gym (Dennison & Dennison, 1992) is a program that involves plenty of movement to pump blood to the brain.

Being cognizant of how brains work and the repercussions of climate and social interactions, we can create a classroom where students feel safe to take risks and make mistakes and know that we are all there to learn. These things lay the foundation for brain friendly learning that will motivate students without controls, punishments, or bribes.

2

The Science of Motivation: The SEEKING System

When educators have opportunities to learn more about the neuro-science of learning and memory, they see immediate applications to the classroom. Stress, poverty, lack of play, and many other factors can all have a negative effect on a student's school experience. The more teachers understand about how brains learn naturally, the more brain-friendly techniques will become the norm and the more frequently students will experience success. One of the promising frontiers of educational neuroscience lies in understanding our basic emotions.

Understanding Our Ancient Brain Systems

The work of affective neuroscientist Jaak Panksepp is rooted in study-ing our most ancient brain systems (Panksepp & Biven, 2012). These systems are ones that we share, via evolution, with other mammals. In the 1980s many educators became familiar with the *triune brain model* originally described by Dr. Paul MacLean from the National Institute of Mental Health in the 1960s (Hart, 1983). MacLean's evolutionary theory proposed that the human brain was in reality three brains in one (see Figure 2.1) and that each worked almost independently of one another and was "in charge" of certain behaviors.

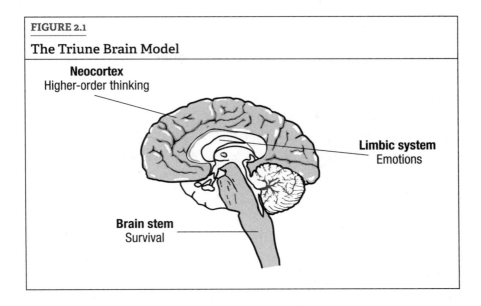

FIGURE 2.1

The Triune Brain Model

- The brain stem—reptilian or dinosaur brain—common to all vertebrates, in charge of survival and the fight, flight, or freeze reflex, is located at the base of the brain
- The limbic system—also known as the Paleo-mammalian brain—common in mammals where social and nurturing behaviors are generated, is located in the midbrain area
- The neocortex—the cerebral cortex, the most recently evolved and most developed in primates where higher-level thinking occurs, takes up the most area in the brain

Although now most neuroscientists agree that MacLean's three-brains-in-one theory has many limitations, this simplified model served as a great introduction for the lay community to understand different brain regions. Even MacLean later emphasized that all aspects of the entire brain were "elaborately connected." In *Human Brain and Human Learning* (1983), author and educator Leslie Hart used the model to introduce important aspects of his "brain-based" education model to teachers (see also Hart, 1981).

Although MacLean's triune brain model ultimately lacked "anatomical precision," Panksepp was drawn to the evolutionary arrangement of the brain and MacLean's interest in studying animal neuroscience to better understand human emotions and behaviors (Panksepp & Biven, 2012, p. 67). Panksepp refers to his refined model as a "nested brain hierarchy" (see Figure 2.2). It is a way of looking at the brain and its layers and how they developed over the course of evolution. Although humans go back several million years, the development of the emotional part of the brain goes back much further, all the way to the time when ancestral mammals evolved from reptiles. These ancient feeling states of curiosity, expectancy, and motivation are initiated in the lowest levels of the brain. In humans they help us to survive as well as to forge new memories that are eventually generated in the higher brain layers.

Recent research using the most advanced brain-imaging technology is helping neuroscientists understand the neural mechanisms for human emotions. By first studying the emotions of other mammals, researchers (e.g., Panksepp & Biven, 2012) have determined there

FIGURE 2.2

Nested Brain

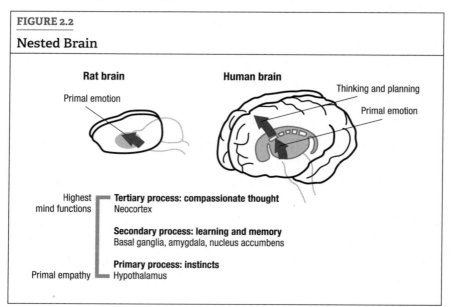

Rat brain

Human brain

Primal emotion

Thinking and planning

Primal emotion

Highest mind functions — **Tertiary process: compassionate thought**
Neocortex

Secondary process: learning and memory
Basal ganglia, amygdala, nucleus accumbens

Primary process: instincts
Primal empathy — Hypothalamus

are seven very basic, primitive emotional processing systems generated in the oldest area of our human brains. This redefinition of the basic human emotions at the primal levels can help us understand what we currently define as "motivation."

Seven Primary Emotional Networks (Processing Systems)

Panksepp has labeled the most powerful of the seven systems as the SEEKING/EXPECTANCY system, and it includes *curiosity, interest, foraging, anticipation,* and *craving.* The other emotion systems (always printed in uppercase to highlight their primary-process evolutionary organization of brain and mind, per Panksepp) are FEAR, RAGE, LUST, CARE, GRIEF, and PLAY (Panksepp & Biven, 2012). The same types of neural pathways and neural chemistry that arouse each of these emotions are found in approximately the same areas of the brain within the various mammal species. Of course, the emotions felt by a dog are not exactly the same as a human's, and we should not expect them to be, but they are evolutionarily related. But by stimulating particular regions in the ancient subcortical regions of the brain, scientists are able to generate similar feelings and reactions in both humans and other mammals.

The seven primary systems include our raw emotional feelings, our instinctual emotional behaviors, and how our bodies move and react as each system is activated. They are not identical in their size or range. They do not work completely independently of one another. Each of the seven basic emotional systems can be located within every mammal's brain, in the same anatomical regions below the cortex and containing the same neurochemical controls.

Panksepp refers to the first four as the "blue-ribbon" core emotions. They are based on well-organized, consistent patterns of behaviors when the corresponding brain region is stimulated. These are inborn capacities of our brain. They are present at birth and are not dependent on life experiences for development, even though they control a great deal of learning and brain development. If, for some reason, these systems are damaged, consciousness itself is compromised.

The "Blue Ribbon" Core Emotions

1. **SEEKING—Expectancy.** When the nucleus accumbens and lateral hypothalamic areas associated with the SEEKING system are electronically or chemically stimulated along a vast circuit known as the medial forebrain bundle (MFB), all animals exhibit intense urges to seek, expect, investigate, and be motivated. The specific feeling is not *pleasure* but intense *enthusiasm*. The specific neurotransmitters (or neuromodulators) associated with each emotion have also been identified. Dopamine is one of the main brain chemicals released when we are seeking, anticipating, and being motivated.

2. **FEAR—Anxiety.** When the amygdala and periaqueductal gray (PAG) areas of the brain are stimulated, the fight, flight, or freeze reaction will quickly emerge. Depending on the degree of the perceived threat, the response may range from cowering to running away in terror.

3. **RAGE—Anger.** When the medial area of the amygdala (and closely interconnected areas in the hypothalamus and brainstem) is stimulated, animals propel themselves forward to fend off the offensive object, and snarl or bite at perceived opponents.

4. **LUST—Sexual excitement.** This primary emotion is generated by other regions of the amygdala and distinct anterior regions of the MFB within the lateral hypothalamus. When animals are in the throes of lust, they exhibit courting behaviors and eventually attempt to culminate in mating behaviors. The tension of this emotion can become negative if satisfaction is elusive!

Additional Primary Emotions

5. **CARE—Nurturance.** When this system is aroused, an animal has strong impulses to tenderly take care of another. It is a major source of our human emotion of love. This primary emotion is generated in vast subcortical systems that include hypothalamic regions of the MFB, as well as many other intervening brain regions reaching

upward to the anterior cingulate cortex; this positive social feeling is fueled by the neurotransmitters oxytocin, prolactin, and opioids.

6. **PANIC/GRIEF—Sadness.** This primary emotion is often triggered by separation from caretakers and feels very distressing—psychologically painful. When people and animals are enjoying secure affectionate bonds, they have a relaxed sense of contentment. When separated from the comfort of a caregiver or when experiencing psychological abandonment, they will react with crying and sadness at the loss. This system runs from midbrain areas through the medial thalamus and to anterior cingulate regions. It is closely intermeshed with the CARE system.

7. **PLAY—Social joy.** This primary emotion is characterized by playful and light-hearted movements and laughter. It is a friendly enjoyment of interaction with others. This system, like all the others, is subcortically situated in ancient brain regions that include the medial thalamus and various other lower brainstem areas.

The SEEKING System: The "Granddaddy" of the Emotional Systems

Affective neuroscientists have spent decades mapping the location of the emotional systems of the brain that are shared by all mammals. Panksepp refers to the SEEKING system as the "granddaddy of the systems," because it is critical for the operations of many other systems, including LUST, CARE, PLAY, as well as HUNGER and THIRST. This crucially important set of primary emotions is the motivational system that stimulates all kinds of exploratory and foraging behaviors critical for survival. Survival needs are the ultimate trigger. The SEEKING system allows all mammals to find and eagerly anticipate the things they need for basic survival, such as food, a mate, and shelter. It is the instinctual drive that all mammals need in order to thrive. Our brains are wired to constantly restore *homeostasis*, the drive to maintain physical equilibrium. Homeostatic imbalances occur when we experience a lack of food, water, warmth, and other requirements for survival. Our brains trigger an urge to seek what we need in order to restore balance. The SEEKING system is in charge of maintaining homeostasis, but it also keeps us motivated and intensely interested in exploring our world, to learn as well as survive. It energizes our behaviors and attitudes, and Panksepp believes that it generates all motivation.

This natural SEEKING system is a primary emotional processing system that energizes our behaviors and attitudes. It plays a key role in learning and making connections. Panksepp believes the *seeking* urge needs to be conceptualized as an emotional system that generates the enthusiasm which underlies all positive motivation. This system (also known as the SEEKING-EXPECTANCY system) keeps us motivated and intensely interested in exploring our world. The EXPECTANCY part of the name reflects that this system helps create anticipatory eagerness in all domains, including the thirst for knowledge.

Rather than working under the construct that our reward system is triggered when we complete a task or finally achieve our intentions, the theory is that the SEEKING system provides us with continued enthusiasm, interest, and motivation while we are in the midst of processing incoming information that is important to us. We feel good while we are *doing* the task, not just upon its completion. Dopamine provides us with a continued feeling of "wanting" as we seek, investigate, and research, and this is a desirable, even *pleasurable* feeling. Survival needs are the ultimate trigger, as every creature strives to find (and eagerly anticipates) the things they need for basic survival. Dopamine increases our general level of arousal, inquisitiveness, and goal-directed behavior as we seek to fill those requirements.

The Role of Dopamine: Neurotransmitter of Motivation

Dopamine is often described as the "power switch" because it energizes and invigorates individuals in relation to their environment. It is the mammalian motivational engine that each day gets us out of bed (or, for other mammals, out of their den or hole) to venture forth into the world. The dopaminergic pathway, part of the medial forebrain bundle, was previously referred to as the brain's "reward system" because it was believed that the release of dopamine caused us to feel pleasure when we met our goal or received the reward. In laboratory experiments, a "reward" was usually something that the subject would work for, such as food or drink. In behavioral neuropsychology, rewards are primarily thought of as "objects or events that increase the probability, and the intensity of behavioral actions, leading to such objects: rewards make you come back for more" (Kaplan & Oudeyer, 2007, p. 227). According to Wright and Panksepp (2012), "It is currently increasingly understood that this 'rewarding system' does not generate sensory pleasure but, rather, a psychomotor eagerness to obtain resources that can engender pleasure and also help avoid various forms of distress" (p. 5).

The pleasure that is felt is the good feeling one has in looking forward to something good, not the pleasure of obtaining something good. Researcher J. D. Salamone concurs with Panksepp that dopamine is responsible not for pleasure but for motivation (Salamone & Correa, 2002). It makes us excited when we think we are going to get what we need. Both Panksepp and Salamone have found that low dopamine levels caused animals to take the "path of least resistance" and not accept a challenge. For example, animals with low dopamine will not run for rewards in a maze, although if placed in the goal box they will consume as much as normal animals. So dopamine has more to do with increasing motivation, focus, and attention than enhancing pleasure.

The latest research confirms that the release of dopamine actually causes us to experience anticipation, excitement, desire, arousal, and the need to pursue and search. "This is a system that urges us to actively—proactively—engage with the world in order to find the resources that we need to thrive as well as to avoid dangers and threats" (Panksepp & Biven, 2012, p. 142).

We as educators can affect the dopaminergic pathway of our students by providing opportunities for them to use strategies that they enjoy as well as to reflect on their experiences to recognize positive involvement with learning. The brain naturally continues to seek dopamine-releasing activities and situations so that we feel good in an enthusiastic, life-affirming way, but this process needs to be guided by insightful educators (see Chapter 5). In contrast, we can also lower dopamine release by creating negative experiences and conditions for our students. Thus, the more we can do in our classrooms to increase the chances of a correct response, the more likely it is that that our students' brains will be motivated to continue (Galvan, Hare, Parra, Penn, Voss, Glover, et al., 2006). If we experience a drop in dopamine related to a disappointing error or mistake, we SEEK to avoid this in future situations. We naturally seek positive reinforcement and avoid negativity. If students receive a dopamine release, accompanied by a positive enthusiastic feeling, they are more likely to persevere through the next challenge and continue to be engaged (O'Doherty, 2004).

Wanting and Liking

When triggered, the SEEKING system generates enthusiastic excitement and anticipation. These behaviors are referred to as *appetitive;* they describe the euphoric excitement we feel as we anticipate meeting our survival needs. This expectancy feeling is entirely different from the pleasure of *consumption* that is felt when we have found the necessities to meet our needs. This SEEKING system is believed to generate and sustain curiosity and motivation. Once we have "found" something needed, useful, or interesting, we become satisfied and temporarily stop further seeking. The latest research shows that it is the opioid system (separate from dopamine) that makes us experience pleasure and feel "rewarded." This was first shown by Panksepp for social rewards that mediate social bonding. It was later found to apply to other rewards as well. According to Pecina and Berridge (2013), the dopamine system is the "wanting" and the opioid system is the "liking." The wanting system gets us into action, and the liking system makes us feel satisfied so that we temporarily stop seeking. Research shows that the dopamine system is the one that leads enthusiastic appetitive behavior, while the opioid system registers the satisfaction of gaining various specific rewards. Thus, in education we need to encourage productive seeking as much as the satisfaction of goals achieved.

The SEEKING System's Three Processing Systems

The SEEKING system has three basic processing levels (Wright & Panksepp, 2012). Understanding how each works will be of great help to classroom teachers. This book will take each one and illustrate how educators in classroom situations can enhance the likelihood of students developing curiosity, perseverance, and tenacity. Students' brains are programed to "seek and find," and teachers can enhance this need by planning strategically to engage the SEEKING system to maximize motivation.

The evolutionary three-level perspective of the SEEKING system helps us understand how an innate drive can lead to anticipation of future events, and ultimately to enthusiastic motivation and problem solving. The first most basic is called the *primary processing system*. The SEEKING system coordinates all incoming sensory information and generates an urge to see what resources might be available. When interactions with objects begin and discoveries are made, the *secondary processing system* launches and learned behavior begins. The *tertiary processing system* is the most advanced level of thinking and learning. As we grow and explore our environment, each of these systems is an integral part of the learning process, but the secondary and tertiary levels will not work without the primary level.

Primary Processing

The very basic emotions emerging from deep in the brain that are instinctual, ancestral "memories" are what all mammals need in order to survive and are the essence of the primary processing system. These urges motivate us to seek out, find, and acquire all the resources we may need to survive, without any formal teaching. It is the inner drive that keeps us moving forward, foraging, and enthusiastically investigating our environment. Beyond meeting our basic needs, we also are highly attracted to anything *novel* in the environment. Without any expectation of rewards, we vigorously explore everything and everyone around us. This is "the basic impulse to search, investigate and make sense of the environment" (Panksepp, 1998). Panksepp says it's like a "goad without a goal," at least initially (Panksepp & Biven, 2012).

Secondary Processing

The foraging and exploration generated by the SEEKING system ultimately produces interactions with the environment. When resources are found and we are rewarded with nourishment, pleasure, play, social interactions, and new knowledge, our brains begin to make new dendritic connections. In essence, we are learning the benefits of *seeking.* The "wanting" system described by Pecina and Berridge (2013) would be considered a secondary process because there must have already been prior experiences that generated a "reward." The memory of the experience and outcome prompts the SEEKING system to continue to pursue a particular path, because there are memories of a pleasurable or satisfying prior experience.

Neuroplasticity describes how firsthand experiences reorganize our neural pathways, resulting in long-lasting changes in the brain's circuitry (Diamond & Hopson, 1998; see Figure 2.3). It was once believed that as we aged, the brain's networks became fixed. In the past two decades, however, an enormous amount of research has revealed that the brain never stops changing and adjusting.

Learning, as defined by Tortora and Grabowski (1996), is the ability to acquire new knowledge or skills through instruction or experience. Memory is the process by which that knowledge is retained over time. The capacity of the brain to change with learning is plasticity. So how does the brain change with learning? According to Drubach (2000), at least two types of modifications occur in the brain with learning:

• A change in the internal structure of the neurons, the most notable being in the area of synapses

• An increase in the number of synapses between neurons

FIGURE 2.3

Neural Pathway

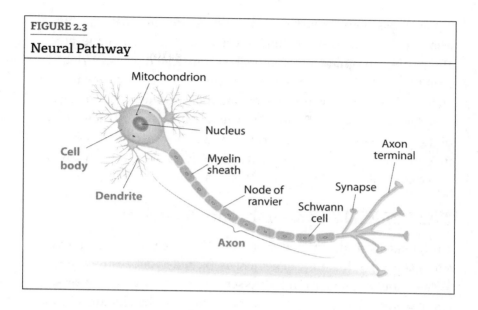

Now the generalized SEEKING system begins to anticipate possible rewards and resources. The brain begins to *learn* that certain conditions and cues may be worth investigating because it remembers great results from past interactions. This appetitive motivation and goal-oriented behavior occurs when the brain has memories and wishes to re-create the reward or experience.

If educators apply this understanding to the design of learning environments, students might experience greater anticipation and motivation. In a later chapter, we will explore how instructional design can be infused with opportunities for firsthand experiences and be based on motivating students by making connections to prior learning.

Tertiary Processing

The primary process drives are instinctual, unconditioned, and survival based. The secondary processes are when true learning begins to take place. Brains are growing and making connections as we are adapting to the environment, maximizing resources, understanding patterns, and developing memories. In humans, the development of the cerebral cortex allows us to think and make connections at much higher levels. This tertiary processing develops with maturity, but it is also our ability to begin to think beyond the present, imagine, create, synthesize, and make cognitively sophisticated plans (Wright & Panksepp, 2012). Other executive functions in the neocortex include complex thinking, organizing, keeping track of time, strategizing, hypothesizing, and combining knowledge and ideas into new possibilities. In Chapter 5, we will provide suggestions for how educators might orchestrate classrooms and instruction to promote creative thinking, problem solving, and other 21st century skills.

The SEEKING System in the Classroom

For humans, this desire to search is not just about meeting our *physical* survival needs. Humans can get just as excited about abstract rewards as they can for tangible ones. Panksepp notes that the system seeks and is attracted to novelty and the anticipation of having fun, playing, and winning (achieving success). "It is evident that the SEEKING-EXPECTANCY system is a general-purpose system for obtaining all kinds of resources that exist in the world, from nuts to knowledge, so to speak" (Panksepp & Biven, 2012, p. 103).

In addition to prompting us to enthusiastically search for resources to meet our basic physical and emotional needs, the SEEKING-EXPECTANCY system also allows (urges) us to do the following:

• experience the exciting feelings of *sustained anticipation* as we look forward to positive experiences and pleasurable activities;

• develop *strategic thinking* and *higher mental processes* as we create hypotheses, make predictions, and fine-tune our expectations;

• promote *optimistic behavior patterns* based on our memory of *prior successful experiences* that create a want-to-do, and a can-do feeling;

• engage in things that might make us *feel important, influential, powerful,* and *honored by our peers;*

- satisfy our attraction to *novelty* and *discrepancies.* "When a stimulus ceases to be novel (when the animal becomes accustomed to it) the SEEKING system no longer responds" (Panksepp & Biven, 2012, p. 106).

When we get thrilled about the world of ideas, about making intellectual connections, about making meaning, it is the SEEKING circuits that are activated. If, in fact, the SEEKING system underlies all positive motivation, tapping this system would be a key to success in classrooms. If educators can stimulate this system into action, they can trigger students' instinctual urge to get out there, do something, find answers, and learn!

Part II

SEEKING in the Classroom:

A Framework for Motivation

3

Exploratory Investigations: Level 1—The Need to SEEK

The SEEKING system begins each day. We forage for our needs from the moment of waking. Finding clothes to wear and food to eat satisfies the SEEKING system and stimulates dopamine release. We have a need to seek. Dopamine fires each time we seek. If you can't SEEK, your life is compromised and you are not happy. The SEEKING system is also shut down when our natural instinct for attachment is violated.

Likewise, if the PANIC-GRIEF system is activated as a result of social disengagement, no learning will take place. The SEEKING system, when activated through social interaction, will directly foster feelings of enthusiasm. PLAY—one of the primary processes that allows us to interact with others in a positive way—helps us achieve prosocial programming for higher brain regions (i.e., in the neocortex) to be engaged. PLAY naturally fosters enthusiasm that could be labeled "social joy." There is a symbiotic relationship between SEEKING and PLAY.

When the SEEKING system is engaged and fueled by dopamine release, we are encouraged to forage, explore, and investigate with curiosity, interest, and expectancy. To activate the SEEKING system in the classroom, educators need to create conditions for it to flourish, including:

- Enriched environments
- Collaborative activities

- Unstructured, spontaneous play
- Recognition of students' needs and preferences
- Time to explore and make choices

Engagement Through the Information-Processing System

Engagement happens as the senses explore the environment until something grabs one's attention. The information/memory processing system has three parts: sensory, short-term/working, and long-term memory (Baddeley, 1996, 1997, 2003, 2007). See Figure 3.1 for an illustration.

The Sensory System

The sensory system acts more like a sieve than a sponge. Because we are bombarded with multisensory input at any given time, we are selective about what we give attention. In fact, we do not respond to 90 percent of stimuli available. Novel or interesting or threatening stimuli are more likely to garner our attention. If there are colorful visuals, interesting or startling sounds, things to examine (tactile), even things to smell and taste, one of these will draw our attention. The sensory memory has a very short "shelf life" of about 3 to 5 seconds, so we must quickly engage students with interesting sensory stimuli so that the primary stage of their SEEKING systems is activated. Then we can be more skillful in moving to short-term working memory to continue to engage their attention and rehearse new content and skills (the secondary processing level).

Short-Term Working Memory

When the primary SEEKING system is activated with sensory prompts and interest develops, the information moves to short-term working memory (McLeod, 2008). Working memory has limited space and time. We are conscious of the information in working memory. Information will not linger, so if we don't use it, we lose it. Therefore, information in working memory needs to be rehearsed. Elaborative

FIGURE 3.1

Information Processing and SEEKING System

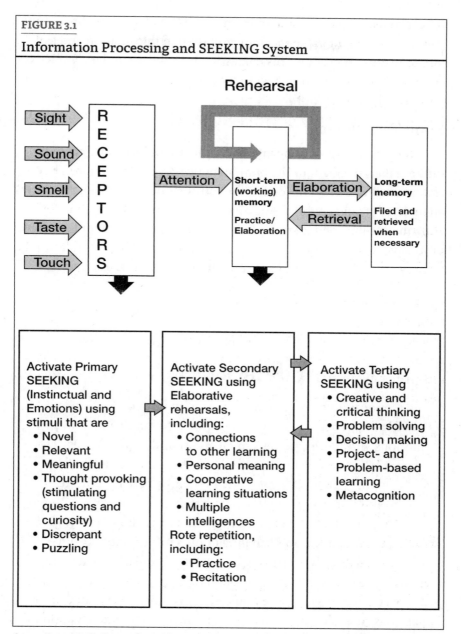

Source: Parts of this figure adapted from *Designing Brain Compatible Learning*, by G. Gregory and T. Parry, 2006, Thousand Oaks, CA: Corwin and from *Building the Reading Brain* by P. Wolfe and P. Nevills, 2004, Thousand Oaks, CA: Corwin.

rehearsal using many instructional methods gives students opportunities to practice and make meaning and to send information and skills into long-term memory. This corresponds to the secondary SEEKING system where real learning takes place and dendritic growth occurs in new neural pathways.

Long-Term Memory

Once information, concepts, and skills are in long-term memory, they are filed throughout the brain in networks of association. They can be retrieved when needed in the future if they have been rehearsed enough for strong neural connections to be developed (myelination). Humans use knowledge stored in long-term memory to build on, solve problems, make decisions, and plan for the future. This is similar to the tertiary SEEKING system where executive functions are activated.

The Hippocampus

The hippocampus, located in the midbrain limbic area, is particularly important in forming new memories and connecting emotions and senses, such as smell and sound, to memories. The hippocampus acts as a memory indexer by sending memories out to the appropriate part of the cerebral hemisphere for long-term storage and retrieves them when necessary.

Bringing out stored long-term memories related to the topic, opening mental files, and bringing known information to consciousness gets brains working and creates "hooks" on which to graft new learning. The hippocampus spends a great deal of time comparing new ideas to previously learned ones. When new information is received, the brain begins to organize the information in working memory. It compares and contrasts patterns and details to make sense of new ideas.

The hippocampus is responsible for turning short-term working memory into long-term memory. It appears that some of this is done during REM (rapid eye movement) sleep. When new information is received, the learner tries to organize it in the working memory. If it is unfamiliar, the learner tries to find a pattern, details, or similarities to something they have previously learned or experienced. The hippocampus tries to weave new information with prior knowledge, changing it into a long-term memory (Geake, 2009).

How to Engage Sensory "Attention-Getting" Memory and Activate the Primary SEEKING System

Novelty

Novelty through a variety of options will get the brain's attention. Laughter, for example, is of great use in the classroom. It relieves tension and stress, raises endorphins, sends oxygenated blood to the brain, boosts the immune system, and creates an episodic memorable experience. Tapping into as many senses as possible is bound to catch more learners. Using a cartoon, picture, music, or a YouTube video to capture interest related to the topic is a good way to get attention and sometimes a laugh. It can be a great discussion starter or raise questions and diverse opinions.

A question or challenge is also an attention grabber. It engages the brain and activates the SEEKING system to problem solve or seek to find an answer. Using think-pair-share (Lyman & McTighe, 1988) to discuss possibilities in a low-risk environment is a good way to keep all brains engaged. Consider this example: The teacher shared the opening paragraph of *A Tale of Two Cities* (Dickens, 1859/1998) on the whiteboard:

It was the best of times, it was the worst of times, it was the
age of wisdom, it was the age of foolishness, it was the epoch
of belief, it was the epoch of incredulity, it was the season of
Light, it was the season of Darkness, it was the spring of hope,
it was the winter of despair, we had everything before us, we
had nothing before us, we were all going direct to Heaven, we
were all going direct the other way—in short, the period was
so far like the present period, that some of its noisiest author-
ities insisted on its being received, for good or for evil, in the
superlative degree of comparison only.

The teacher then asked students to find a partner and discuss these
ideas: Why did the author use these contrasts? Is it the same today?
Why do you think so? Prompting dialogue with one other person
allows students to feel safe, so they will risk ideas and opinions. Everyone is engaged.

Curiosity

The brain is naturally curious, and offering puzzles or conflicting
or discrepant events will cause the brain to begin SEEKING answers
or solutions.

A principal was observing a student teacher in a 3rd grade classroom. She was preparing to teach a science lesson about matter. The
children were coming in from recess and hanging up their jackets.
Miss Brown was wearing a white lab coat, goggles, and latex gloves.
She was also looking worried. The children looked at her curiously
and asked if there was a problem. She told them she had a big problem and they asked her to share it. They sat down quickly and were
all eyes and ears. She pulled a plastic baggie of a mixture referred to
as oobleck (a cornstarch and water mixture that exhibits a variety of
characteristics—feeling at times firm and at others spongy) out of her
lab coat pocket and held it up. She showed the children and explained
that she had found this and didn't know what it was. They were very
interested and she had their rapt attention. This was her introduction

or anticipatory set for her science lesson—far more interesting than starting with "Boys and girls, today we are going to learn about matter." That introduction wouldn't have "mattered" as much to them as the mystery she created. They were ready to learn and wanted to know.

Rich Resources and Realia

In 387 BC, Plato advised educators not to force-feed their students.

> Elements of instruction . . . should be presented to the mind in childhood; not, however, under any notion of forcing education. A freeman ought not to be a slave in the acquisition of knowledge of any kind. Bodily exercise, when compulsory, does no harm to the body; but knowledge which is acquired under compulsion obtains no hold on the mind. (Plato, n.d./ 2009, p. 226)

Even that long ago, Plato had a vision of quality learning. He believed that "stand and deliver" or forced learning was not the way to go. Without connections, relevancy, and meaning, new learning would not be retained. The natural SEEKING system is ready and waiting to do what is necessary given inviting, challenging situations.

Providing materials and resources so students can explore and find out what they know about the topic or discover what they are interested in can capture their attention. Have students conduct an Internet search to add to their background knowledge or use other virtual technology to familiarize themselves with a topic, process, or location.

If we pay attention to Piagetian stages of development, we sometimes forget that it is not just 7- to 11-year-olds who need to have concrete representation of concepts or ideas. Even into adulthood the concrete stage can be a good beginning. Social studies students can examine authentic memorabilia from pioneer days and guess their use and identify what we use today for the same task. Manipulatives in math engage, capture attention, and deepen understanding.

Relationships Are Essential

Humans are social beings, and the need to connect is innate. Abundant research supports this idea. Gopnik, Meltzoff, and Kuhl (1999) remind us that everyone comes with a "contact urge." People seek to be in the company of others. We crave inclusion. Hallowell (2011) says that if we are not able to interact with others daily, we are actually losing brain cells, while those who do engage others grow brain cells.

To illustrate the effect of peer support, Robert Sapolsky (1998), an American neuroendocrinologist and professor at Stanford University, observed primates and how they reacted in a group situation. If there was undue stress and friends were around, the stress was lessened. If the primate was in a threatening, unsupportive group, the stress was magnified. If the group was inclusive and supportive, the stress was less traumatic for the primate. We all need social support. This is true in classrooms as well. The current outburst of bullying creates a very stressful and unfriendly climate in schools and classrooms. For empathic students, even if they are not the ones being bullied, it is very stressful to see others treated so badly. Their learning brains suffer, too, living in these harsh conditions. Their concern with physical and emotional well-being preoccupies their attention and learning is blocked.

Collaboration Fosters Peer Relationships

Our innate need for belonging is a catalyst for cooperation and sets a good stage for interactive exploration.

Evidence that the need for belonging (although not studied as much as other needs) may drive the other needs such as power, achievement, intimacy, and approval is provided by Baumeister and Leary's (1995) research. They suggest that belonging is as compelling a need as food, and human culture is conditioned to attain it. Evolutionarily the small group was needed for survival. It is a feedback loop: cooperation fosters belongingness and belongingness leads to cooperation.

Several researchers support the value of cooperative interactions in the classroom. Vygotsky (1978) proposed that we learn through interactions with knowledgeable and more capable colleagues. Collaboration gives students an opportunity to feel important, influential, powerful, appreciated, and honored by their peers.

In a review of cooperative learning, Shachar and Sharon (1994) found that cooperative structures enhance students' intrinsic motivation, leading them to learn more in small groups than in large groups. Cooperative learning motivates students' achievement, peer interaction, problem solving, and decision making, and engages the SEEKING system.

"One behavioral indication of student motivational involvement is the proportion of their class time they spend on-task," which is also referred to as "engaged time" by Slavin (1990, p. 64) in reference to group work. Doing beats listening when it comes to engagement. Students are also motivated when they receive signs from peers that they are safe and valued (Wasserman & Danforth, 1988).

Cooperation and the Brain

Cooperation actually activates the reward system in the brain and increases the release of dopamine so that we feel good. Another positive, feel-good neurotransmitter, oxytocin, is released during social bonding and trust development. Given the diversity in heterogeneous classrooms, students don't always gel as a group. To build community in the classroom, teachers can use team-building strategies. Class or group composition is not nor should be homogeneous. Group combinations can vary by chronological age, background experiences, cultures, strengths, and needs. It is the heterogeneous composition that broadens perspectives and brings diverse thinking to the group (Lou, Abrami, & d'Apollonia, 2001). Students learn from people at different stages of readiness and capability, and when working together can complement and enhance one another's learning.

Cooperative group learning has been ranked high on the list of instructional strategies that increase student achievement (e.g.,

Cawelti, 2004; Johnson & Johnson, 1981; Johnson, Johnson, & Holubec, 1998; Marzano et al., 2001). The Visible Learning resources and research of John Hattie (2009) also place cooperative group learning high on the list of impactful strategies for student learning.

For group work and learning to be successful, students may need to develop the required social skills to work together.

Tribes: Building Community

Jeanne Gibbs (2006), in her 30 years of working with the concept of tribes, realized that students need help to successfully work with others. Just because students are put in a group to complete a task does not mean that their work together always goes well. Conflict occurs because of lack of social skills, tolerance, and task management. The Tribes program is focused on developing a respectful community of learners who learn about each other so that respect and tolerance can grow, bound together by four shared norms or agreements:

- **Attentive listening:** to be able to listen with ears, eyes, and heart to another without interruption or judgment and to check for understanding
- **Appreciation/no put-downs:** to be kind and show appreciation in words and deeds without negative remarks, hurtful names, gestures, or other behaviors
- **Right to pass:** to have control over the level of participation; to observe, listen, and offer ideas voluntarily or when asked
- **Mutual respect:** to affirm and value the individuality of each person

The Tribes program also provides many simple community builders that can be done with students to help forge understanding and bonding among class members. These activities reinforce and strengthen the four agreements. Excellent resources are available for elementary, middle, and high school classrooms.

The following are several examples of quick activities adapted from Tribes programs that can be done to build and foster community in the classroom.

The Observers

After a group works together, have them reflect on the process. Have them shut their eyes and "rewind the video" in their mind. Ask them to reflect on the following:

- Who got you started with the task?
- What was your part? How did you help the group?
- Whom did you appreciate?
- Did everyone participate?

When students finish thinking about the task, they could

- write a journal entry about the group process;
- tell someone in the group what they appreciated; and
- set a team goal for next time.

Finding Gold

Ask the students to write down three things they do well or strengths they have. Have them do a walkabout and share their strengths with another student, complimenting the other student on his or her strengths and perhaps adding one from their perspective. Then ask them to move on to new partners.

Build a Time Capsule

Ask students to do a quick-write about what is going on in their world today and the world in general. In a community circle, ask students to share one of the things they would put in a time capsule, or create a bulletin board and post their cards (without their names). Students can read the cards when they have time and identify who they think wrote the card.

Classroom Norms

Sometimes teachers involve students in developing classroom norms so that they have meaning and ownership for all students. Ask students what norms are important to them in school and in the classroom. Giving them a voice and then listening and acting on their needs gives them a sense of emotional, psychological, and cognitive safety. This trusting environment lessens the chance for stress and anxiety and prevents cortisol (stress hormone) release. Without the "reflex response" in a stressful environment, students are more motivated to keep working on tasks without fear of failure and within an atmosphere of peer support. Their ability to focus and problem solve is greater as they are working in the prefrontal cortex and not in the fight, flight, or freeze mode.

Opportunities for Unstructured PLAY with Others

PLAY—defined here as vigorous positive engagement with others—is considered one of the seven primary emotions. While it may seem unusual to refer to PLAY as an emotion, what if we called it "social joy" as the affective scientists do? How might opportunities to PLAY and experience joyfulness with others influence motivation?

As one of the primary emotions studied by Panksepp, PLAY and joy are most associated with socialization and bonding with others. The emotional vocalizations humans make often convey their feelings to others. There are growls and yells of RAGE, cries of PANIC, and soothing whispers and tender words of CARE. Likewise, PLAY promotes laughter, giggles, and even shrieks of joy.

By identifying the areas in the brain that generate the PLAY response from lab animals, researchers have been able to stimulate (either by regulating the neurochemicals or by using an electrical deep brain stimulator) the region and produce joy and a PLAY response in the animals. While it may be difficult to determine whether or not the rats were "happy," researchers were able to record the increase in dopamine and endorphins as a result of the stimulation. These areas of primary emotions are located in the same places in rats' brains as they are in human brains.

Jaak Panksepp is known as the "rat tickler." While researching the seven primary emotions in lab rats, he stimulated the PLAY area in their brains through neurochemical and deep brain stimulation (electricity). Panksepp also believed that perhaps good old-fashioned tickling could generate the PLAY emotion and joyousness. By placing ultrasensitive microphones near the cages, he was able to record the happy squealing that rats vocalize when being tickled by the researcher. Not only did the rats love being tickled, but they continued to SEEK out *more!* Whenever the tickling would stop, the rats would run back and nudge the hand for more. The joy of play and being tickled was a strong motivator!

Psychiatrist Stuart Brown (2009) was collecting data on the effects of play around the same time. He had been studying "play histories" of thousands of individuals to determine how the role of play (or the lack of play) in childhood and adulthood affected their lives. To learn more about *why* people play, he turned his research to the animal world. He interviewed National Geographic Society researchers Bob and Joanna Fagen. When he asked, "Why do animals play?" Bob replied, "Because it's fun!" Later he added that in a world where one is constantly working on surviving, play provides a way to practice life skills that might be needed in the future.

Play and the Brain

Many researchers have determined that unstructured, spontaneous PLAY is a crucial developmental element (Brown, 2009; Diamond & Hopson, 1998; Panksepp & Biven, 2012; Ratey, 2008).

• Animals that play a lot learn how to navigate and adapt and are smarter.

• Animal species that play a lot generally have larger brains.

• Active play stimulates the release of BDNF (brain-derived neurotrophic factor), which stimulates nerve growth in the brain, particularly in the amygdala.

• Lots of play correlates to the development of the frontal cortex.

• Lots of play also increases growth in the cerebellum. The cerebellum was once thought to be primarily responsible for motor control and coordination, but recent research shows it is responsible for attention and language processing.

- Playing with toys and socializing in an enriched environment can prompt brain growth and development.
- Playing *feels* good. When people seek out opportunities and others with whom to engage in play, anticipation causes a dopamine release. Research indicates that it is our endogenous opioid and cannabinoid receptors (our brain's natural pleasure chemicals) that are triggered to provide us with a feeling of euphoria and the giggles. This feeling can be somewhat "addicting" and may be why some children (and adults) just can't get enough play time!
- Playing provides a way to practice, restimulate, and strengthen new neural connections (see Chapter 4).

While animals may use rough-and-tumble play to practice fighting or determine a pecking order, young children also use these interactions to discover their own strengths and learn what others can tolerate. Brown (2009) even links a lack of rough play in young children to potential bullying behaviors later on. "Playful interaction allows a penalty-free rehearsal of the normal give-and-take necessary in social groups" (Brown, 2009, p. 32). Without an opportunity to practice and find out what "hurts" another person, they may grow up not recognizing the natural signals one might make to demand someone stop hurting them. Through play, children can learn the difference between friendly teasing and mean-spirited bullying and how to let the aggressor know their feelings.

In the animal world as well as with humans, play teaches how to socialize successfully. It is when playing with others that one develops emotional intelligence, discussed earlier—the ability to perceive others' emotional state and to learn appropriate responses (also known as social intelligence; Goleman, 1995).

Practicing skills needed for the future doesn't have to be boring or tedious. If you make a game of something, you can be getting better and have fun doing it. Playing allows for mistakes without heavy consequences. Most important, for our discussion here, opportunities to PLAY can be a terrific motivator.

The urge to PLAY and to SEEK out others for some enthusiastic social fun are natural primary process emotions. If young animals are healthy and feeling good, they almost invariably play together when given the chance. "Play only occurs when one is safe, secure and feeling good, which makes play an exceptionally sensitive measure for all things bad" (Panksepp & Biven, 2012, p. 355).

The urge to play boisterously is so strong in many young children that parents, teachers, and caregivers may discourage it. Many researchers are gathering data suggesting that attention disorders and hyperactivity may be a result of diminished opportunities for physical play. Richard Louv in his book *Last Child in the Woods* (2005) suggests that a lack of specifically outdoor play influences the likelihood of attention deficit. He has coined the term "nature-deficit disorder." The simple first response to managing students with ADHD might be to consider more frequent outside and rough-and-tumble play opportunities (Panksepp & Biven, 2012; Ratey, 2008).

> We believe that if the power of PLAY is well recruited in our educational systems, especially at the pre-school level, we will be able to reduce the all-too-frequent diagnosis of ADHD. Given the potentially deleterious long-term effects of psychostimulants like Ritalin, we suggest that children might better learn to control themselves in classrooms and assimilate academic material, if they start the day with half an hour of active play. (Panksepp & Biven, 2012, p. 383)

It is important to note that true PLAY comes from children's imaginations and minds. It may not have set rules or be structured so that there are winners and losers. It may appear purposeless to the adults present. In a classroom, setting aside some space, time, and opportunities for play could provide great benefits. Incorporating play in the classroom

- satisfies the natural urge children have to SEEK out fun and to socialize with their peers.

- provides a fun way to practice new knowledge, procedures, and understandings.
  - creates a natural way to build important social skills.
  - builds community and diminishes social isolation.
  - stimulates brain growth and development at any age.
  - motivates students who are hyperactive or struggling with attentional disorders.
  - relieves stress and tension and allows for greater focus immediately following opportunities to play.

In some educational or therapeutic settings, additional playtime may be used beneficially as a motivational "reward" for academic progress. (See the next section on Preferred Activity Time.)

Preferred Activity Time

Preferred Activity Time (PAT) is a system where students are able to spend time having fun while learning after earning the privilege (Jones, 2013). A standard format is to set aside 10 to 20 minutes for PAT.

Here's an example of what a teacher might say to set the stage for the PAT activity:

> "Of course, once you get started on an art project, you always love to have more time. And this time, you can! All the time we save during the day by hustling will be added to PAT. We could have 40 minutes for art if we really get things done."

This example gives students motivation to push them to earn the extra time.

PAT can also be used in secondary classrooms. Perhaps the teacher spends 10 minutes each day orally summarizing the important facts that the students needed from the day's lesson. Instead of losing the students' interest every day, the teacher might turn the same amount of time into a quiz show-style game. Students might want to have a few minutes before the quiz show starts for a short group review—a peer tutoring session. The students could earn extra game time if there were quick transitions and efficient cleanup. Knowing that there is a fun, clever (and sometimes a student-chosen) activity to look forward to can be a great motivator. Students might begin to SEEK out how they could earn more time for PAT. Jones maintains that the PAT time does not have to be a daily activity for it to be an effective motivator.

Discovering Students' Strengths and Interests

Although we know that some brain functions are inherent in all brains, we also know that every brain is uniquely wired by nature (genes) and nurture (environment and experiences). Most brains follow a normal developmental trajectory. Each is also idiosyncratic in its strengths and weaknesses for learning particular types of information (Geake, 2009). In other words, what event or activity will cause an appetitive dopamine release in one brain may not do so in the brain sitting next to it in class. Blakemore and Frith (2005) suggest that teaching in the future may mean just offering learners appropriate opportunities and encouraging them to partake. Therefore, it is necessary to recognize that different brains have different preferences.

Cognitive psychologists have long suggested that people fit into different learning styles, yet neuroscience does not support this notion (Sousa &Tomlinson, 2011). However, we all have preferences for how we learn and different stimuli that increases our dopamine levels when we anticipate different options and choices, given prior successes and enjoyment. These choices often reflect not only things we enjoy but also those we can accomplish without undue stress. The challenge for teachers is to differentiate options for rehearsal of content and skills, as well as to use differentiated authentic assessments that allow students to demonstrate competencies.

However, we don't want a heightened awareness of students' strengths and weaknesses to lead us to label students or cater to their needs, or to limit their experiences as a result of this awareness. As Howard Gardner (2006) points out, our learning profile is as unique as our thumbprint, but our profile can change and evolve over time, whereas our thumbprint doesn't. The best route for teachers is to offer choices and a good variety of options so students can choose from something that will engage them and also help them learn. When we go fishing, what do we put on the hook—what we like or what the fish like? It only makes sense to use multiple lures to attract and hook all the learners.

We can use many tools to identify preferences in visual, auditory, tactile/kinesthetic modalities (Dunn & Dunn, 1987; Gardner, 2006), and style delineators from theorists such as Gregorc (1982) and Silver, Strong, and Perini (2000). Inventories and surveys are abundant on the Internet for teachers to use; just search for "multiple intelligence inventories" or "learning style inventories." Here are a few examples:

- V-A-K Learning Styles Survey
  - http://nwlink.com/~donclark/hrd/styles/vak.html
  - www.brainboxx.co.uk/a3_aspects/pages/vak_quest.htm
- Multiple Intelligences
  - www.literacyworks.org/mi/assessment/findyourstrengths.html

To thoughtful teachers, learning preferences and styles are "not a method of restrictive teaching, but a reminder of the benefits of explicit mixed modality pedagogy" (Geake, 2009, p. 75).

Explicit Mixed Modality Pedagogy

An abundance of evidence- and research-based studies look at instructional strategies and approaches that have an impact on student achievement. *Research based* refers to a meta-analysis of research available, and *evidence based* looks at results of classroom/teacher implementation of those strategies. Marzano et al. (2001) offered nine instructional strategies from a meta-analysis (research based) that had promise in increasing student learning with percentile gains ranging from 22 to 43. After teachers used these strategies (evidence based), specific techniques for their implementation emerged (Dean, Hubbell, Pitler, & Stone, 2012).

These strategies were extremely "brain-friendly" as they aligned with how the brain prefers to learn and what it finds interesting, such as the need for social interaction, patterns, visuals, clear expectations, meaning and relevance, and SEEKING. They also offered a great variety of ways to process information, practice skills, and use higher-order thinking, as well as to satisfy the variety of learning preferences and multiple intelligences of students. Gordon Cawelti (2004) edited a handbook with top strategies that cross a variety of curriculum areas, as well as those specific to different subject disciplines. John Hattie (2009) also provides an extensive meta-analysis on instructional strategies suggesting the effect one can expect with the use of each one.

Many of the strategies from all the studies overlap. Some best practices are as follows:

- Clear objectives and purpose
- Ongoing feedback
- Recognizing effort and providing recognition
- Cooperative group learning
- Reciprocal teaching
- Questions, cues, and advanced organizers
- Generating and testing hypotheses
- Recognizing similarities and differences
- Concept mapping
- Meta-cognitive strategies
- Creativity programs

Accessing Prior Knowledge

Also related to student interest is the prior knowledge they bring to the new learning. Pre-assessing students' capabilities lets teachers know what students already know, what they are interested in, and what gaps there are to fill, so there is a foundation on which we can attach the new learning. Sometimes in pre-assessing we realize that students have "burning questions" that set up the appetitive SEEKING system. (See more on making a connection to prior learning in Chapter 4.)

Giving Students a Voice

In order for students to feel safe and included, things that are familiar and interesting to them need to be incorporated into the curriculum. It is amazing how incorporating personal information and likes and dislikes into learning can engage students who would otherwise be disengaged.

Giving students a voice in the classroom creates an environment that seems tailored to the learners. A teacher might ask students to complete a brief exit card to share what they enjoyed about the day's class, what was difficult for them, or perhaps what they would like to do to better meet their learning needs. The teacher can then incorporate these ideas, if possible, in the next day's tasks not only to engage students at a deeper level, but to continue to develop trust. This reciprocal process where the teacher asks and responds to student wants and needs has a powerful effect on students' self-esteem and also builds in the opportunity for freedom and the power to influence their learning.

Quaglia and Corso (2014) contend that student voice has a great impact on student learning. In Quaglia's work, thousands of students were surveyed about their aspirations, identifying their hopes and appreciation for what was important to them in schools and classrooms. Quaglia has shared eight student aspirations and materials on the Qisa website (www.qisa.org/framework/students.jsp).

Quaglia and Corso share three principles: self-worth, engagement, and purpose. The eight student aspirations are listed and explained under the three principles.

Self-Worth

When students know that they are important members of the class/school community, they can flourish. They need people they can trust, learn with and from, and who believe that they can be successful.

- Belonging: being part of the group, but special as well
- Heroes: relying on people who are there and believe in you

- Sense of accomplishment: having people recognize you and your accomplishments, including effort

Engagement

Engagement entails being fully involved in the learning process and being enthusiastic and willing to take steps forward.

- Fun and excitement: having a joyful outlook no matter what you are involved with
  - Curiosity and creativity: questioning the world you live in
  - Spirit of adventure: being excited to venture forth, risking and trying new things

Purpose

Having purpose means acting confidently and responsibly in the present but looking forward to careers and the future.

- Leadership and responsibility: being accountable for decisions made
- Confidence to take action: setting goals and planning to reach them

In many classrooms, teachers ask students for feedback and open the door for student voices to be heard. However, hearing is not enough. Truly listening and then taking these ideas and suggestions to heart when planning and organizing learning needs to be the next step. Information alone changes nothing. We need to take action regarding their feedback and needs. They are our clients and we are professionals who need to respond. They have great ideas about how to change schools and how learning could be enhanced. When students know that they are being heard and responded to, they will be far more engaged as their needs are being met and their self-worth and efficacy will be increased. Educators need to ask the right questions, respond to the best suggestions, and respect student needs in order to engage and intrigue.

Use student surveys to ask them what they enjoy or prefer in class, the types of activities they appreciate, and the things they struggle with. Exit cards asking them to describe details of the learning experience as "Clear as glass," "A little fuzzy," or "Clear as mud" will also give you information that allows you to check for understanding or adjust learning for student preferences or needs.

Personal Interest in Students

Students are more than just a "student." Each student is a whole person, who likes to be recognized for many things in his or her life. It is useful to get an idea of what students do outside school, including sports teams, musical interests, family events, games, and friends. The more we know about our students, the more we can appreciate them, relate the learning to their real world, and comment on their interests to better forge strong relationships (Combs, 1982; McCombs & Whisler, 1997). Often negative behavior results from students who don't feel noticed or welcome (Sheets & Gay, 1996). Studies show that teachers who exhibit consideration, patience, and buoyancy are more likeable and, as a result, have better relationships with students (Barr, 1958; Good & Brophy, 1995).

Showing a personal interest in students is important, costs nothing, and requires little planning. Connect with students by using some of the following suggestions:

- Greet students by name as they arrive.
- Chat informally, before, during, and after class.
- Take an interest in extracurricular activities.
- Interact during lunch.
- Recognize and comment on other events in their lives such as drama, sports, and musical interests.
- Compliment them on out-of-school successes.
- Ask about their health if they have been absent. Acknowledge that they were missed.

Make sure you are being somewhat equitable with your attention by considering the following:

- Provide wait time for all students.
- Make eye contact.

- Use proximity to be close to all students at some time in the classroom in the power zone.
  - Acknowledge their ideas and show appreciation.
  - Encourage involvement and seek out their thoughts.

TIME to Explore and Make CHOICES

In early elementary classrooms, time to play is generally not an issue that has to be addressed. However, with the emphasis on Common Core State Standards and universal testing, some kindergartens look less like play-based programs. Teachers have replaced student-directed learning with more direct instruction and drill in math and language to get students ready for the tests. Preschool and kindergarten teachers are very adept at offering multiple venues for youngsters, full of curiosity, to explore and investigate in classrooms that are more student centered and led. Studies have shown that Ontario (Canada) children in full-day play-based kindergartens have better vocabularies, reasoning skills, and general knowledge, as well as stronger communication and social skills. Brownell and colleagues (2015) say that although children in a full-day program are two to four times ahead of others in several key learning skills by grade 1, this impact doesn't make any significant difference by the time they get to high school as they spend more and more time in grades 1 to 8 in traditional "sit and get" academic programs.

Teachers observed that some 1st grade students are expected to sit at their desks for long periods of time after spending two years in play-based kindergarten. These students want to explore answers to questions and issues they are interested in, rather than being teacher driven. The improvement in their engagement is the most powerful aspect—children are completely engrossed in everything they do in the classroom and anticipate the next day with enthusiasm. Teachers have found that students are much more involved as active participants in their own learning process. It's not about educators filling up "empty vessels"; it's about students coming with questions and ideas and learning alongside the teachers.

4

Learning and Anticipation: Level 2—SEEKING and Making Connections

Setting up a safe and secure classroom that is filled with novel opportunities and promotes exploratory investigations is the first step in orchestrating a brain-friendly teaching and learning environment. The SEEKING system will thrive when inviting, interesting, multisensory experiences are abundantly available. When students get to experience a multisensory enriched environment, learning will be inevitable. How might we maximize learning and extend the initial understanding once a learning experience has occurred? This chapter will investigate the second processing level of the SEEKING system where memories are formed and clever educators can create anticipation to build student motivation.

The human brain contains more than 100 billion neurons, each with a cell body, a trunk-like axon, and multiple dendrites that can branch out and grow with stimulation. Neurons communicate with one another through electrochemical interactions. At the synapse, the point where one dendrite connects with another, neurotransmitters are released, stimulating the receptors to continue a chain reaction of "firing off." *Brain plasticity*, also known as *neuroplasticity*, is a term that refers to the brain's ability to change and adapt as a result of experience. Until the 1960s, researchers believed that changes in the brain could only take place during infancy and childhood. By early adulthood, it was believed that the brain's physical structure was permanent. More recent research has demonstrated that the brain continues to create new neural pathways and alter existing ones in order to adapt to new experiences, learn new information, and create new memories.

Neuroscience researcher Eric Kandel (2006) was awarded a Nobel Prize in Medicine in 2000 for his early discoveries about neuroplasticity and memory. Known as the father of the biology of learning and memory, he discovered that when people learn something, the wiring in their brains changes. When the brain is exposed to multisensory stimulation in an enriched environment, neurons are prompted to grow dendritic branches and form new synaptic connections with other neurons. Neuroscientist Marian Diamond proved that environmental enrichment could influence and change the structure of the brain by increasing the dendritic connections and density in the cerebral cortex (Diamond & Hopson, 1998). Although there are sensitive growth periods for children, her work indicated that being exposed to enriched environments and stimulation could enrich brains at any age.

Current research shows that brain growth and development are shaped by three factors:

- the interaction among genes,
- the environment, and
- our experiences.

The National Scientific Council on the Developing Child (NSCDC, 2007) notes, "The brain is composed of billions of highly integrated sets of neural circuits (i.e., connections among brain cells) that are 'wired' under the interactive influences of genetics, environment and experience" (p. 6). A child's genetic makeup (nature) is equally influenced by the environment and experiences it has (nurture).

When children enthusiastically explore their environments, they are actively building their brains' neural networks. Each encounter, every interaction, triggers their brains not only to make a new connection, but also to notice and record what happens into their working memories. Young brains are particularly sensitive to sensory input and enriched environments. As explained in the previous chapter, classrooms that promote curiosity, exploration, play, and investigation are promoting the growth of new neural circuits. This innate primary processing level of the SEEKING system begins to build a foundation for the secondary processing level, where our experiences can be elaborated and expanded to form new memories.

From "Unknowing" to Knowing

Researchers in affective neuroscience describe conscious learning as the point at which we move from innate primary processing to secondary processing. When we are SEEKING at the primary process level, we are not *consciously* trying to learn and are intrinsically motivated to enthusiastically explore and investigate, or to avoid and flee if necessary. This dynamic is referred to as *anoetic* consciousness, or without explicit knowledge. This type of consciousness is in the here and now and requires no higher-level thinking or reflection. This "constitutes a critical antecedent that is foundational for all forms of knowledge acquisition via learning and memory, giving rise to a knowledge-based, or noetic, consciousness as well as higher forms of 'awareness' or 'knowing consciousness'" (Vandekerckhove, Bulnes, & Panksepp, 2014, p. 1). When we have sensory stimulation and feedback from an experience or action, we begin to develop a *noetic* consciousness, a "knowing about the world." When an experience gets intense enough or proves to be of value, we can describe and reflect on it. This recognized awareness is the beginning of the learning process.

Early learning specialists also emphasize the importance of adult interaction and conversations with infants and young children, a process known as "serve and return." Facial expressions, vocalizations, and gestures help young children begin to shape an understanding of their world. When a young infant gazes or points at an object (the "serve"), the caregiver immediately provides feedback (the "return") about the object by naming it, describing it, pointing, bringing it closer, and so forth. Every time the child initiates interest (using her own SEEKING urge), she is provided with immediate interaction and feedback that generates even more interest. This can help develop continued motivation to explore.

When interacting with infants and young children, parents, teachers, and caregivers can facilitate learning by "returning" feedback:

- Verbalizing—naming the object, telling what it is and what it does
- Vocalizing—using intonation, adjusting the volume level, creating sound effects
- Demonstrating—showing the object and what it can do and how it works
- Gesturing—pointing or using hand or facial gestures
- Classifying—identifying what type of object it is and other, similar things

Children raised with this kind of attentive interest and quick response may demonstrate continued motivation and curiosity. Remember, *they* have been the initiators of the interactions.

What if we were to continue this "serve and return" model with students in school? When students demonstrate interest in something, we can provide additional information and a brief description. As students mature, we might just provide a jump-start or steer them in a direction for them to do their own research and investigations. The key here is that students must have time and opportunities to explore and become curious. When the curriculum in a classroom is strictly dictated, there are few chances for students to be curious and investigate—to initiate and be in charge of their own learning.

In addition to being "in the moment" and learning from an experience and its accompanying emotional messages, humans are also capable of *reflective consciousness*, or the capacity to have thoughts about experiences, as well as thoughts about thoughts, and an "awareness of awareness." Most researchers believe this ability is probably unique to humans. It allows us to transform thoughts and our remembered experiences into an autobiographical perspective. As a result of having an experience, these developing understandings and memories can now help us function at higher levels of thinking. We can remember and access past experiences and begin to anticipate future events.

As previously stated, the "wanting" system described by Pecina and Berridge (2013) is part of the secondary processing system. The memory of a past experience and previous outcome prompts the SEEKING system to continue to pursue a particular path, because there are memories of a pleasurable or satisfying prior experience. Prior experiences that generated satisfaction or a "reward" now create anticipation and we start SEEKING for different reasons. We *liked* what happened, so now we *want* to re-create the experience.

"Active Processing" with Multiple Rehearsals

When a new synapse is made between neurons, it is very fragile and tenuous. Each time the experience is re-created or recalled, the neuronal firing strengthens the dendritic connection. When cells are prompted to communicate frequently, the connection between them is strengthened. When these messages travel the same pathway in the brain, the transmissions become faster and stronger. When they are repeated frequently, the pathway becomes more automated. Hebb's Law "Neurons that fire together, wire together" has been attributed to the work of neuropsychologist Donald Hebb (1949). When something is practiced enough, it can become a pattern. We are able to automatically recall an action or memory with just a little prompting. This is key to more complex learning. Knowing math facts and combination patterns allow us to do higher-level computations efficiently. However, it is also possible to learn and practice something incorrectly, resulting in the wrong pattern being stored in the brain!

Classrooms must be designed to facilitate multiple opportunities to do *active processing*. Processing new learning in a variety of ways, multiple times over several days, and discussing it with others will build long-term memories and deepen learning. If the initial experience is relevant, meaningful, fun, novel, and exciting, the learner will gladly SEEK to do it again and again.

We can encourage the secondary processing system in the classroom by

- discussing new learning experiences;
- making a connection to prior learning;
- discovering relevance to students' daily lives;
- creating sustained anticipation and interest; and
- developing optimistic "growth" mindsets.

The remainder of this chapter will explore each of these strategies.

Discussing New Learning Experiences

A teacher, parent, sibling, or peer can be a helpful guide, facilitating a child's initial experience, providing interaction, and encouraging continued interest. Russian psychologist Lev Vygotsky (1978) suggested that children continue to attend to things in the environment that are the biggest and loudest until they learn how to use "mental tools." By developing these "tools of the mind," children begin to learn how to examine experiences in a more purposeful way. In the beginning, the interactions with others will lead to an internalization of a dialogue and reflection questions to pose about new learning (see www.toolsofthemind.org/philosophy/vygotskian-approach/).

Determine "Aha!" Moments

Be ready to point out an observation that may have slipped by a student's realm of current understanding. Adults can instil a sense of wonder, awe, and excitement by reacting to experiences as they happen and bringing attention to the moment. Look for the "Wow!" and "Aha!" moments, and don't be afraid to interject.

- Wait a minute. . . . Did you see that?
- Wow! That was really something!
- That surprised me—how about you?

Ask Reflection Questions

As a child has a new experience or an "Aha!" moment, a clever "guide on the side" will be ready with open-ended questions to promote a more in-depth look at the interaction. Modeling questions, encouraging thoughtful reflection, and inspiring extended thinking will help to build the tools of the mind.

General questions can be about pertinent terminology. For young students, this develops a broader vocabulary related to the experience.

- Do you know what this is called?
- Do you know why they call it _____?
- Can you guess what they call this part?

In *Visualizing and Verbalizing,* Nanci Bell (2007) suggests helping children focus on the gross and fine **details** to help them begin to form *concept imagery,* the ability to create an imaged gestalt (whole). This is the underlying sensory-cognitive function needed for reading comprehension and critical thinking. Questions can be asked about the big picture (whole) and then about more specific structures (details):

Gross Details	Fine Details
What?	When?
Size?	Background?
Shape?	Movement?
Number?	Mood?
Color?	Perspective?

More questions might help a child understand **procedures** by discussing how something works.

- What do you think happened first?
- I wonder what will happen now?
- Do you know how this works?

It may be helpful to dialogue about some **generalizations.**

- Do you think it is always like this?
- Is this the same as _____?

- So what do you think is the big idea?

Generate questions to promote a discussion about **problem identification.**

- What's going on here?
- Is it *supposed* to do that?
- What could make this be more successful?

Ask Essential Questions

To encourage creative problem solving and to add depth to new learning, consider introducing and integrating the elements of essential questions, as described by Jay McTighe and Grant Wiggins (2013). "These are questions that are not answerable with finality in a single lesson or a brief sentence—and that's the point. Their aim is to stimulate thought, to provoke inquiry, and to spark more questions, including thoughtful student questions, not just pat answers" (p. 3). They are provocative, generate discussions, and often prompt more questions. They can help uncover depth and richness of an experience rather than just understanding the face value.

What makes a question "essential"? According to McTighe and Wiggins, questions that meet all or most of the following seven criteria qualify as essential:

A good essential question
1. Is *open-ended;* that is, it typically will not have a single, final, and correct answer.
2. Is *thought-provoking* and *intellectually engaging*, often sparking discussion and debate.
3. Calls for *higher-order thinking,* such as analysis, inference, evaluation, prediction. It cannot be effectively answered by recall alone.
4. Points toward *important, transferable ideas* within (and sometimes across) disciplines.
5. Raises *additional questions* and sparks further inquiry.
6. Requires *support* and *justification*, not just an answer.

7. *Recurs* over time; that is, the question can and should be
   revisited again and again.
(McTighe & Wiggins, 2013, p. 3)

Share Findings with Peers

Creating opportunities for learners to share and discuss their
thoughts and ideas is a key element of active processing. Vygotsky's
(1978) theory of child development emphasizes *social constructivism,*
the need for interactions between children and their social environment in order to acquire the tools of the mind. Many strategies for
quick pair-shares can be used to encourage students to interact with
each other.

- **Pair-share:** Also called think-pair-share (Lyman & McTighe,
1988) or timed-pair-share (TPS), this is a collaborative strategy where
students (1) think about an idea, problem, or reading passage; (2) meet
with a partner; and (3) share their ideas with one another and perhaps
arrive at an answer.

- **Study buddies:** Students may have chosen each other or teachers may have assigned a "buddy" with whom students can work or
study during certain activity times. Buddies might be determined in
advance using appointment cards or clock partners.

- **Elbow partners:** Quick opportunities for a brief discussion can
be conducted with the person sitting right next to each student. The
student nearest to one's "elbow" becomes the buddy with whom to
chat or discuss.

- **Discussion dots:** In small groups of three to five students, provide each student with a strip of colored sticky dots. Each student has
his or her own unique color. As the student makes a comment or contributes to the conversation, he or she puts one of the sticky dots onto
an index card in the middle of the table and may not make another
comment until each of the other students has contributed remarks.

Write in Reflection Journals

Encouraging students to write about an experience in a reflection
journal also stimulates active processing. Entries don't need to be

lengthy descriptions or explanations. Quick opportunities to reflect on experiences in writing allow the brain to process and note the new learning in a different way. Consider these techniques:

- **One-minute quick-writes:** Students are asked to write as much as they can about the topic or activity in just one minute. Add extra challenges such as "Try to include as many vocabulary words from this week as possible" or "Include another person's perspective on this topic."

- **Twitter message:** The ultimate short summarization is to create a Twitter post of no more than 140 characters that can be sent to the classroom hashtag or physically handed in as students leave (i.e., a "Twexit card"). Try a quick message posted to a digital noteboard such as Padlet or Wall Wisher.

- **Delayed response:** An easy and quick assignment is to ask students to reflect on the classwork later in the day: "After you've had time to think about it, write down your thoughts about today's activity in your reflection journal."

When bringing an experience to a close it can be helpful to **summarize** the new learning. While the interaction may have had multiple layers and episodes, see if students can wrap it up in a summary statement.

- So what is the big "take-away" from today?
- What three words would you use to describe what we learned today?
- If someone asked you what you learned today, what would you say?

Making a Connection to Prior Learning

Going from the unknown to the known may happen in a split second. It is the moment when a new experience or observation triggers a *connection* to a prior understanding. Helping students make a connection to prior learning is a powerful teaching strategy. Use the following ideas to guide students to find connections.

• **Recall of past experiences:** Teachers can frame a new learning opportunity by helping students recall past experiences. It may be reminding them of something that was done in class or the previous year. Asking questions to determine if this is something they have experienced outside school will help them see the connections.

• **Metaphor and similes:** A simile directly compares two things because they share a common feature. The word *as* or *like* is used to compare the two examples. Asking students to compare the idea or experience to something else provides a way for them to connect the unknown to something already known.

  – How is this *like* what we did yesterday?
  – Is this *like* anything you have seen before?
  – Where else have you seen something *as* _____ *as* this?
  – What parts of this is *like*_____?

Analogy

Thought requires concepts, and analogies are perhaps the best way to gradually understand a concept. Analogical thought associates common elements between an understood concept and one that is not yet understood. Thus, the analogy "A heart is like a pump" can help students understand what a heart does to maintain blood circulation if they have seen and understand what a pump does to regulate water circulation. Hearts and pumps are not the same thing conceptually, but they can be analogous to each other. When scientists think about an analogy, they seek to make even closer connections. These may eventually lead to new discoveries and improved technologies, which lead to further analogies. Analogies thus represent an important part of how human society evolved.

Our ability to understand, create, and communicate analogies is perhaps our most definitive cognitive property. Beyond science and technology, analogical thought provided the basic creative spark that led to advances in such other fields as the arts, religion, and government. It is probably what separates us cognitively from primates and other social mammals.

Many children's stories, fables, parables, and proverbs are analogous because children have to develop an understanding of many complex and often moralistic concepts. For example, we tend to use the Santa Claus parable with children at a very early age. They soon discover that the gifts actually came from their family. They then learn to give their own gifts at Christmas and birthdays and to share toys with siblings and friends throughout the year. By the time they reach adulthood, we hope that they will have mastered the complexities of philanthropy, from tipping for some services to writing a check for a charity.

Analogies are figures of speech that are so wrapped up in the fabric of our social species that we often do not realize how many we confront and how easily we understand them. Much of our conversation includes metaphors, similes, and hyperboles. Analogical songs and stories are often expanded into films, TV shows, and plays. Child play and professional sports are analogical. In *As You Like It*, William Shakespeare suggested:

All the world's a stage,
And all the men and women are merely players;
They have their exits and their entrances

Source: Some ideas from *Understanding and Mastering Complexity* (2014). R. Sylwester & D. Moursund, Eds. Eugene, OR: Information Age Education. ©2014 Moursund & Sylwester. A good current book on analogy is by Douglas Hofstadter and Emmanuel Sander (2013), *Surfaces and Essences: Analogy as the Fuel and Fire of Thinking.*

Discovering Relevance to Students' Daily Lives

"Why do we need to know this?" Almost every teacher has heard that question from a disengaged student at some point. Yet it may be the most poignant query that any student can ask! There's no disagreement that sometimes the academic skills that are to be taught and learned at school can become tedious and lack an obvious purpose. Many students (and teachers) may not be able to explain *why* the lesson is important or what the ultimate goal is for learning the concept or skill. Students will be more motivated to stick with a learning activity if the goal of the lesson has obvious relevance and value. This isn't new information, but we can better understand the reasoning if we review the neuroscience behind the theory. Understanding the SEEKING system and *incentive salience* may help us better determine why students must see relevance in what is being presented.

> The anticipatory eagerness aroused by SEEKING is more future-opportunity oriented than the sensory affects. It is ready to capitalize on all the environmental resources needed for survival. In that general role, it was "designed" through evolution to be the most general-purpose emotional system of the brain. (Wright & Panksepp, 2012, p. 5)

As we learn about the SEEKING system, we discover that dopamine is being generated on a regular basis to maintain a general feeling of interest, curiosity, and enthusiasm. This ongoing state is called *tonic dopamine levels.* We are always on the lookout for access to possible survival needs, as well as human interaction and possible opportunities for PLAY and fun. This means that our senses are constantly scanning our environment for possible cues about potential "rewards." Some researchers believe that unconsciously this process keeps our working memory quite taxed, as we are constantly "looping" information through our frontal cortex and reviewing data. Our brains are comparing what we are seeing, hearing, and noting in the environment with what we have stored in our memories about their respective value to our needs. We are always *en garde*, ready to react, move, and take action if we notice a cue that might trigger a response (Chatham, 2007). This future-oriented wanting (a reward) circuit responds to any survival-sustaining activities and is referred to as being in an "appetitive state."

When we have had some experiences in the world, we begin to learn and file the information into our long-term memory for future reference. As cues emerge regarding a possible valuable, survival-related opportunity, our dopamine system triggers a transient "phasic" burst of the neurotransmitter. Encountering *relevant* stimuli causes short-term activation of dopamine cell firing. Our brains shift into a *consummatory* state as our behaviors change into eating, drinking, playing, and socializing—enjoying the rewards of our SEEKING behaviors. "[We discovered that] the system was a goad without a fixed goal, which was used for the SEEKING of all rewards and, gradually, with learning, expectancies for all rewards" (Panksepp & Biven, 2012, p. 124).

Incentive Salience

Incentive salience is an attribute given by the brain to reward-predicting stimuli. According to Kent Berridge and other researchers, while the SEEKING system is enthusiastically urging us to explore unconditionally, it may also be "wanting" and particularly sensitive to the quality of particular stimuli. Incentive salience changes a simple sensory experience into something that commands our attention and encourages us to approach. This means that some stimuli may have more of a motivational "magnet" quality that makes it a desirable and attractive goal, and causes it to be sought out (Wikipedia contributors, n.d.).

How might understanding incentive salience change what educators do in a classroom? Our students' brains have an urge to explore and investigate, but there is a filter that will heighten the attraction (and motivation) to learn. This filter is always looking for and *wanting* experiences and opportunities that do the following:

- provide for our survival needs right now;
- might provide knowledge and assistance for us in the future;
- make a connection to what we already know and have an interest in;
  - offer opportunities to socialize and connect with others;
  - provide a "call to action" to help others with survival needs (CARE);
  - give acknowledgment about our own cultural background and identity;
  - share an opportunity to be acknowledged and build personal prestige; and
  - provide us time and tools to be creative and to play.

Culturally Responsive Education

Culturally responsive education links curriculum, instruction, and assessment to the students' experiences, language, and culture—in other words, to their prior knowledge. Teachers also can take the time to reinforce prior knowledge through their daily teaching practices by providing students with opportunities to establish both personal and real-world relevance. Many instructors *tell* why the material is relevant, but few actually provide the time and resources necessary to help students assimilate the understanding on their own. In sum, teachers should have two goals:

- All students are able to connect new learning to their prior knowledge and experiences.
- All teachers relate new learning to students' everyday lives and culture.

In the anthology *Mind, Brain, and Education* (Sousa, 2010), the authors show that many studies have documented the importance of relevance. Making connections to real-life situations and problems doesn't need to be limited to content areas. Students can approach even higher-level mathematics courses more enthusiastically if they can observe the application in real-life local and global examples. "The data also revealed that student engagement in learning these statistics concepts is likely to be increased by including real-life local and global examples drawn from everyday life. This project suggests that by incorporating a wider range of examples based in real-life local and global issues in a culturally mixed statistics class, it is possible to engage a wider range of students" (Bhowmik, 2013, p. 293).

As students discover how a particular learning goal or task may have personal value, they are likely to increase their motivation to learn (Kenny, 2010). Demonstrating the relevance of the lesson or activity to real-world situations is important at every level of education. In a study reported in *Active Learning in Higher Education*:

> The interviewees found that teaching abstract theory alone was demotivating. Relevance could be established through: showing how theory can be applied in practice, establishing relevance to local cases, relating material to everyday applications, or finding applications in current newsworthy issues. The traditional building block curriculum, which devotes substantial parts of initial courses to basic theory, could demotivate students if they could not see how the theory was applicable to the discipline or profession. (Kember, Ho, & Hong, 2008, p. 249)

Real-World Applications

- **Local water supply:** A variety of school subjects and concepts can be illustrated by investigating the local water supply, watershed, and water companies. Environmental science, meteorology, statistics, politics, community education, sustainability, and public health are all possible entry points to study an important local survival need.

- **City planning:** The politics of building design, urban planning, environmental issues, and so forth, can all be incorporated as students relate school subjects to local urban planning. For example, after the destruction of downtown Santa Cruz, California, following the earthquake in 1989, middle school students used knowledge of Leonardo da Vinci's city planning designs to submit suggestions to the local city council.

- **Toilets:** While learning about the steam engine, the cotton gin, and other significant inventions, coauthor Martha Kaufeldt once had students study and investigate the history of "everyday objects." The most popular was the toilet! This proved to be a highly motivating topic—with an incredibly relevant real-world application.

Creating Sustained Anticipation and Interest

> Allowing one's self to be puzzled helps generate anticipation of knowing a solution to what is causing the puzzlement/mental discontinuity. The mental discontinuity can function to help create a broader continuity (a larger connected chunk of reality). A student who explores what she finds remarkable, interesting, and important is more wonderfully mentally aroused and engaged. Teacher-telling doesn't help exploration. (Pritscher, 2011, p. 12)

So how does an experience and "knowing" influence our behaviors? Once we have had an "Aha!" moment, will we want to continue to explore and learn even more? We might first look to the field of behavioral psychology where we will find two opposing viewpoints regarding the role of *operant conditioning* on learning.

The Law of Effect

Behavioral psychologist E. L. Thorndike (1932) first described the law of effect in the early 20th century. The law states that *the more satisfaction that is gained from engaging in a particular behavior, the more likely that behavior is to be repeated.* Conversely, *those behaviors that result in a negative or unpleasant experience are likely to occur less frequently.* Later B. F. Skinner developed a subfield of psychology known as operant conditioning, the study of how environmental rewards and punishments influence behavior (Panksepp & Biven, 2012). The law of effect suggests that humans and other animals try different behaviors and assess the outcomes. We will continue to do more of the behaviors that generate better results and less of those with negative or poor results. Feedback will influence our future decisions and behaviors.

In a 2005 interview, Panksepp suggested that the law be referred to as the "law of affect" because it really has to do with how the experience makes us *feel*. He reports that even Thorndike's original description of the law states that "actions followed by *satisfactions* are increased, and those followed by distress are diminished." When satisfaction is achieved when completing a task, the mind moves from an unconscious knowing to a conscious knowing. If students feel a sense of satisfaction upon the completion of a task or activity, they will be likely to SEEK out opportunities to do it again. If the activity brings distress, they will need encouragement and support to try it again. If the satisfaction isn't acknowledged, noted, and brought to the student's consciousness, we may miss an opportunity to build motivation.

As students participate enthusiastically in a task, the SEEKING system is generating lots of feel-good dopamine. There is a sense of satisfaction in simply *doing* the activity. Once the task is completed, the research shows that dopamine is paused and the opioid system releases a brief squirt of euphoria. The SEEKING system then resumes and the cycle continues. The brain begins to make associations and judgments and to determine value and relevance. The higher-level brain function in the neocortex will begin to guide planning and execution to repeat the pleasurable experience. We begin to *anticipate* possible pleasure. Likewise, it may also begin to inhibit actions, delay responses, and be tolerant of frustrations. In most cases, this internal reward system should be enough.

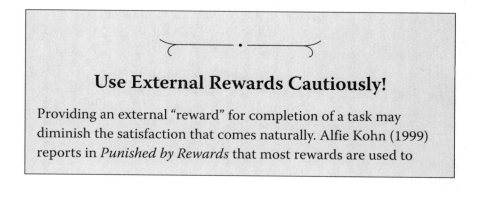

Use External Rewards Cautiously!

Providing an external "reward" for completion of a task may diminish the satisfaction that comes naturally. Alfie Kohn (1999) reports in *Punished by Rewards* that most rewards are used to manipulate behavior. Rewards are most damaging to a student's interest and engagement when the task is already intrinsically motivating. One of the most carefully researched findings in psychology is that the more you reward someone for doing something, the less interest that person will tend to have in whatever he or she was rewarded to do in the first place.

Recent neuroscience research can help provide a better understanding of why an extrinsic reward may reduce intrinsic motivation. The most modern theory is called the "reward prediction error" hypothesized by Wolfram Schultz at Cambridge University (Panksepp & Biven, 2012). Schultz studied dopamine levels in hungry monkeys as they were rewarded with food. The monkeys' dopamine levels were recorded when they were exposed to a flash of light just before getting a food reward. The light always indicated that food was on its way. The monkeys' dopamine levels were at first high when the food arrived. Later the levels were highest just when the light flashed—it was a cue that food would be coming. They were being *conditioned* to expect a reward. However, when the light came on and no food followed, the release of dopamine decreased, they exhibited frustration, and their interest waned—they experienced a reward prediction error. An unexpected reward once or twice at the beginning was motivating and helped refine learning. As soon as the reward was removed, the monkeys knew that the flashing light was no longer a consistent or reliable signal for food, and dopamine levels reduced. When dopamine is reduced, enthusiastic motivation is also reduced.

"There are at least 70 studies showing that extrinsic motivators—including A's, sometimes praise, and other rewards—are not merely ineffective over the long haul but counterproductive with respect to the things that concern us most: desire to learn, commitment to good values, and so on" (Brandt, 1995).

Short-Term Working Memory

> As the cognitive science of the late twentieth century is com-
> plemented by the affective neuroscience of the present, we are
> breaking through to a truly mental neuroscience, and finally
> understanding that the brain is not merely an information-
> processing device but also a sentient, intentional being. Our
> animal behaviors are not "just" behaviors; in their primal
> affective forms they embody ancient mental processes that
> we share, at the very least, with all other mammals. (Solms &
> Panksepp, 2012, p. 25)

As mentioned previously, the first stage of the information processing system begins with the sensory memory hopefully garnering
attention, capturing enthusiasm, and getting the SEEKING system
activated. Having a short attention span, we need to move students
into the WANTING system and then engage their working memory.
Marzano and colleagues (2001) suggest that it might take a learner 24
practice trials to gain 80 percent mastery. It is the working memory
that helps us clarify concepts, internalize, and transfer learning into
long-term memory.

Developing Optimistic "Growth" Mindsets

Carol Dweck's (2006) research has focused on motivation. She
believes that individuals can be placed on a continuum regarding their
personal views of where ability comes from. There are two different
trends of thought. Some believe it is an innate ability that contributes
to their success. This view is referred to as a *fixed mindset* (or entity
view of intelligence) mindset. The second is a *growth mindset* (incremental view of intelligence).

Fixed-mindset students dread being unsuccessful, as it would reflect
negatively on their abilities, whereas growth-mindset students do not
fear failure because they believe that they can improve with effort.

In a fixed mindset students believe their basic abilities, their intelligence, their talents, are just fixed traits. They have a certain amount and that's that, and then their goal becomes to look smart all the time and never look dumb. In a growth mindset students understand that their talents and abilities can be developed through effort, good teaching and persistence. They don't necessarily think everyone's the same or anyone can be Einstein, but they believe everyone can get smarter if they work at it. (Morehead, 2012)

Students with a growth mindset will be more motivated to keep on working despite setbacks. Teachers can teach students about how their brains work and the concept of neuroplasticity that assures them that brains continue to grow and change throughout life even into old age.

5

Imagination and Synthesis: Level 3—Applying Higher Cognitive Processing

The primary process drives are instinctual, unconditioned, and survival-based. During the secondary processes of the SEEKING system, true learning begins to take place. Brains are growing and making connections as we are adapting to the environment, maximizing resources, understanding patterns, and developing memories. In humans, the development of the cerebral cortex allows us to think and make connections at much higher levels. This *tertiary* processing develops with maturity, but it is also our ability to begin to think beyond the present, imagine, create, synthesize, and make cognitively sophisticated plans (Wright & Panksepp, 2012). The brain continues to draw on the SEEKING system, but now it searches for new ideas and systems, and creates innovations by using imagination, creativity, and synthesis (see Figure 5.1).

Understanding the Cerebral Cortex and Executive Function

Higher cognitive processing takes place in the outermost area of the brain called the cerebral cortex. It is the gray matter that is approximately 2 to 3 millimeters thick, composed of ridges and valleys (sulci and gyri), and covers the entire brain. The neocortex (the newest brain

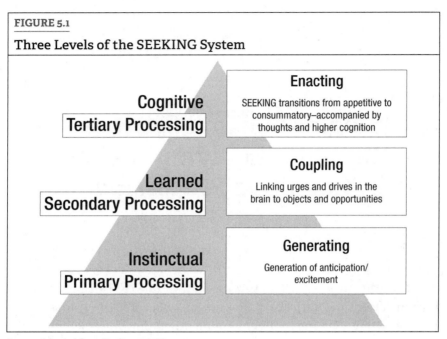

FIGURE 5.1

Three Levels of the SEEKING System

Cognitive
Tertiary Processing

Enacting
SEEKING transitions from appetitive to consummatory—accompanied by thoughts and higher cognition

Learned
Secondary Processing

Coupling
Linking urges and drives in the brain to objects and opportunities

Instinctual
Primary Processing

Generating
Generation of anticipation/excitement

Source: Adapted from Panksepp & Biven, 2012.

region to develop evolutionarily) is six layers deep, contains 10 to 16 billion neurons, and composes most of the cerebral cortex. Main brain regions such as the motor cortex, sensory cortex, and visual and auditory cortex are all part of the neocortex. The frontal lobes are connected to all other areas of the brain and are particularly linked to the midbrain (limbic) area and, specifically, the amygdala.

The prefrontal cortex undergoes the greatest amount of postnatal development. It may be the main area of the brain that truly can be considered a *tabula rasa* at birth. The dorsolateral prefrontal cortex (DLPC) is located right behind the top of your forehead. The DLPC is primarily involved in the development, with experiences and maturation, of executive function. *Executive function* is the term describing a set of thinking and processing skills integral to the development of self-regulation, conscious control, and one's success in life. Often compared to a busy air traffic control tower, executive function includes

- planning and organizing,
- holding multiple ideas and thoughts in working memory,
- strategizing and problem-solving,
- complex thinking and hypothesizing,
- keeping track of time, and
- synthesizing by combining knowledge and ideas into new

possibilities.

As described in Chapter 4, neuroplasticity is the key to the development of the neocortex and executive function. One must have multiple firsthand experiences in order to develop these skills. The conscious control of one's thoughts, actions, and emotions begins at the end of the first year of life and continues to develop through early adulthood—as long as one has opportunities to practice and utilize these skills. Later in this chapter, we will provide suggestions for how educators might orchestrate classrooms and instruction to promote the development of creative thinking, problem solving, and other 21st century skills.

Executive Function and Self-Regulation

Executive function is a group of skills that help us to orchestrate multiple threads of information going on at the same time. With experience and practice, one can develop the abilities to focus, process information, filter out distractions, make decisions, and revise plans as necessary. Acquiring the foundations of these skills is one of the most important and challenging tasks of the early childhood years, and having the right support and experiences through middle childhood, adolescence, and into early adult life is essential for the successful development of these capacities (Center on the Developing Child, n.d.).

When planning and making decisions, one's emotions are always in play. Panksepp refers to the fact that in this tertiary processing level there is "bottom-up" thinking (emotions are influencing our planning and decisions) and "top-down" thinking (our rational minds can calm our emotions) (Panksepp & Biven, 2012, p. 8). During adolescence, bottom-up thinking can greatly influence thinking and decision making. It's been said that teens are like inexperienced drivers trying to steer a car that has been turbocharged by their hormones. When trying to make a decision, they experience a constant struggle between top-down executive function and a bottom-up influence of desires. This internal struggle in an immature brain often makes for some poor decisions.

Higher Mental Processes

With experiences and maturity, executive function has the potential to fully develop. As presented in the previous chapter, research indicates that frequent opportunities to PLAY may be a significant factor in the development and connectivity of the frontal lobes. When young children play, they are beginning to build capacities to role-play, think creatively, and consider other viewpoints—all good foundational skills for executive function. With frequent PLAY good-feeling experiences, memories are formed and children begin to SEEK out *more* of the creative outlet. All are great rehearsals for real-life scenarios.

As mentioned earlier, Pink (2009) suggests that after our basic needs are met, we are driven by three true elements of motivation: autonomy, purpose, and mastery. He believes the secret to high performance and satisfaction—at work, at school, and at home—is our need to direct our own lives, to learn and create new things, and to have opportunities to be of value.

Developing Autonomy and 21st Century Thinking

Self-direction is our natural inclination. We are programmed to be active information seekers. In addition to SEEKING what we need to survive and be happy, we also strive to acquire and understand complex knowledge. Even when we are alone, we have an inner drive urging us to seek out the company of others, explore interesting ideas, fix things, create beautiful art, strive to become healthier, reflect on our feelings, and ponder big ideas. But most important, we want to have real control over our own lives. We feel empowered when we are able to choose what we do and when we do it. Motivation is greatest when we are getting to learn and do what interests us the most.

Can student autonomy be a part of an education? Absolutely! Two shifts will need to happen:

• Students will need to have practice making thoughtful important decisions. They will have to learn techniques for critical thinking, problem-solving strategies, and research skills, as well as skills for working and communicating with others.

• Educational institutions and teachers will have to shift their practices to meet the needs of these 21st century learners. They will have to shift from being a "sage on the stage," a stand-and-deliver and cover-the-curriculum teacher, to a "guide on the side" and an "activator for learning" (Hattie, 2009), designing and implementing a curriculum that supports students' developing true thinking skills.

21st Century Skills

We have entered what many are referring to as the Knowledge Age economy—an information-driven, globally networked era of rapid change and development (Trilling & Fadel, 2009). A huge skills gap is developing in the workplace because the existing educational system is still stuck doing what it has done for 200 years: sharing content and factoid knowledge, from instructors presenting content in a one-size-fits-all approach to instruction. Students leave school to attend university or begin in the workplace, and many soon find that they are lacking the necessary skills to be successful in the digitally connected world.

Teachers must be willing and motivated to become learners, too. We will no longer always be the "keepers of the knowledge." Investigating, analyzing, and problem solving are skills we will need to develop and practice right along with our students. It's been said that "thinking will not be driven by answers but by questions." Educators really can't continue to replicate a mode of teaching that is obsolete in our current era (Pritscher, 2011). We need to have the courage to open our minds to the possibilities, embrace uncertainty, and be ready to be flexible and adaptable as the changes are happening very fast.

These patterns of intellectual behaviors can be taught—or at least encouraged—by intentionally designing environments in which learning is focused on developing students' 21st century skills, or what have also been called "habits of mind" (Costa & Kallick, 2008) and lifelong survival skills. Classrooms that encourage thinking and interactions with real-world problems are highly motivating.

Several models can help us understand the range of skills that we will need to demonstrate and nurture within our students.

Partnership for 21st Century Skills

The Partnership for 21st Century Skills (now known as the Partnership for 21st Century or P21) is a combination of private and public groups that strives to close the "profound gap between the knowledge and skills most students learn in school and the knowledge and skills they need in typical 21st century communities and workplaces" (Partnership for 21st Century Skills, n.d., p. 2). The six key elements of 21st century learning

- emphasize core subjects,
- emphasize learning skills,
- use 21st century tools to develop learning skills,
- teach and learn in a 21st century context,
- teach and learn 21st century content, and
- use 21st century assessments that measure 21st century skills.

The learning skills that should be emphasized include information and communication skills, thinking and problem-solving skills, and interpersonal and self-directional skills. The partnership encourages schools to emphasize three content areas: (1) global awareness; (2) financial, economic, and business literacy; and (3) civic literacy.

Habits of Mind

Originally designed by James Anderson, Art Costa, and Bena Kallick (Costa & Kallick, 2008), the collection of 16 "habits of mind" represent key skills that should be encouraged and developed in all students (see Figure 5.2). With experiences, students can call on different habits and apply them in more effective and strategic ways. As they become more adept, they will be able to recognize opportunities to apply them in novel and complex situations. Continued experiences and successful interactions will build self-confidence. With reflection and metacognitive reflection, students build self-monitoring skills and become more self-directed (Costa & Kallick, 2008).

Seven Lifelong Survival Skills

In his book *The Global Achievement Gap,* Tony Wagner (2008a) proposes seven survival skills that his research has determined as the key to thriving in the 21st century world of work. "These skills are the same ones that will enable students to become productive citizens who contribute to solving some of the most pressing issues we face in the 21st century" (Wagner, 2008b, p. 20).

- Critical thinking and problem solving
- Collaboration and leadership
- Agility and adaptability
- Initiative and entrepreneurialism
- Effective oral and written communication
- Accessing and analyzing information
- Curiosity and imagination

Metacognition and Mindfulness

One of the most important tasks in education is to provide opportunities to teach students how to learn on their own throughout their lifetimes. In addition to developing the higher cognitive skills necessary to thrive in the 21st century, students will also benefit from learning reflection skills such as metacognition and mindfulness. One of the wonderful features of our complex brain/mind system is that because of our well-developed neocortex, we are able to have internal dialogues. We can use our brains as time machines! We can think about

FIGURE 5.2

Habits of Mind

Persisting
Stick to it! Persevering in a task through completion; remaining focused; looking for ways to reach your goal when stuck; not giving up.

Managing impulsivity
Take your time! Thinking before acting; remaining calm, thoughtful, and deliberative.

Listening with understanding and empathy
Understand others! Devoting mental energy to another person's thoughts and ideas; making an effort to perceive another's point of view and emotions.

Thinking flexibly
Look at it another way! Being able to change perspectives, generate alternatives, consider options.

Thinking about your thinking (metacognition)
Know your knowing! Being aware of your own thoughts, strategies, feelings, and actions, and their effects on others.

Striving for accuracy
Check it again! Always doing your best; setting high standards; checking and finding ways to improve constantly.

Questioning and posing problems
How do you know? Having a questioning attitude; knowing what data are needed and developing questioning strategies to produce those data; finding problems to solve.

Applying past knowledge to new situations
Use what you learn! Accessing prior knowledge; transferring knowledge beyond the situation in which it was learned.

Thinking and communicating with clarity and precision
Be clear! Striving for accurate communication in both written and oral form; avoiding overgeneralizations, distortions, deletions, and exaggerations.

Gathering data through all senses
Use your natural pathways! Paying attention to the world around you; gathering data through taste, touch, smell, hearing, and sight.

Creating, imagining, and innovating
Try a different way! Generating new and novel ideas, fluency, originality.

Responding with wonderment and awe
Have fun figuring it out! Finding the world awesome and mysterious; being intrigued with phenomena and beauty.

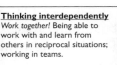

Taking responsible risks
Venture out! Being adventuresome; living on the edge of your competence; trying new things constantly.

Finding humor
Laugh a little! Finding the whimsical, incongruous, and unexpected; being able to laugh at yourself.

Thinking interdependently
Work together! Being able to work with and learn from others in reciprocal situations; working in teams.

Remaining open to continuous learning
I have so much more to learn! Having humility and pride when admitting you don't know; resisting complacency.

Source: From *Habits of Mind Across the Curriculum: Practical and Creative Strategies for Teachers* (p. x), by A.L. Costa and B. Kallick, 2009, Alexandria VA: Copyright 2009 by ASCD.

things in the past and in the future. We can reflect on an experience, analyze it, and make predictions about what might happen in the future. Students could benefit from targeted instruction and demonstrations of how to develop these important skills. *Metacognition* is simply "thinking about thinking." Developing good thinking skills should also include reflecting and analyzing our thinking strategies— thinking about what we know and making decisions about how we might use the new insight to go about learning in the future. When we take time to consider and discuss the strategies that we use to solve a problem, we become more consciously aware of the processing involved in reaching a resolution. It allows us to *construct* our own responses regarding the success or efficiency of a given experience.

John Flavell (1979), one of the first researchers in metacognition and memory, defined the following two areas:

Metacognitive knowledge—awareness of one's thinking

- Awareness of knowledge—understanding what one knows, doesn't know, and wants to know
- Awareness of thinking—understanding the task, being able to identify the problem, and being able to conceptualize what needs to happen first
- Awareness of thinking strategies—understanding the various approaches that might be used to be successful

Metacognitive regulation—the ability to manage one's own thinking processes

- Being able to thoughtfully plan out a task at hand: identify the problem, choose a strategy, organize our thoughts, and anticipate the outcome
- Monitoring our efforts while we are working and learning, evaluating the effectiveness of our strategies
- Checking the outcomes—being able to assess and evaluate the results against specific criteria

In the Classroom

When teachers create curriculum and strategies that help students develop an awareness of their thinking processes and opportunities to reflect on their tasks, students can improve their cognitive skills while gaining subject-matter content. Rather than just learning factoids and trying to "cover content" or comprehend a reading passage, students learn how to reflect, analyze, organize, and evaluate. These experiences help make students' thinking *visible*.

Here are some strategies to include regularly in the classroom—at all grade levels—that will help build metacognitive skills:

- **Predicting outcomes:** Have students predict their thoughts on what strategies they will be using and why.
- **Evaluating work:** After completing a task or project, give students opportunities to assess their work and determine their strengths and areas that still need development. Using a rubric can be helpful.
- **Questioning by the teacher or a significant friend:** "What are you doing now? Why are you doing it that way? How is that helping you?"
- **Encouraging self-questioning:** Classrooms might have sets of reflection questions that are used for different types of activities. Students will begin to internalize these reflection questions.

Mindfulness

Just as it is important to learn how to think about thinking, there is also great value in learning how to think about our feelings, assess our physical health and mental state, and calm our busy brains. This skill is called mindfulness: "paying attention to your life, here and now, with kindness and curiosity" (Saltzman, 2010).

In *Mindfulness: A Teachers' Guide*, Amy Saltzman (2010) suggests that we are often asking students to "pay attention," yet we rarely teach them how to do it. Mindfulness is the ability to pay attention to your internal and external worlds. When you are practicing mindful behaviors, you are taking time to focus on your thoughts and your emotions in the here and now. Recent research suggests that teaching mindfulness strategies in K–12 education may be a key in helping children and adolescents enhance attention, executive function, learning, and prosocial behaviors.

Thinking Taxonomies to Promote Motivation

It was once estimated that 85 percent of the type of thinking going on in many classrooms is at the very lowest levels of cognition. Answering simple questions about basic knowledge and comprehension is too often the extent of the rigor being asked of students and their brains. If our goal is to increase student motivation, it is important to revisit different levels and types of thinking we might use in the classroom. When a novel concept is first introduced, students may express some interest and motivation. Initial understanding, terminologies, and generalizations might be investigated. But then what? If students are able to show basic proficiency, is that it? Our goal must be to extend rigorous thinking and generate tasks that encourage higher-order thinking skills (HOTS) and ultimately motivate the brain's natural urge to learn.

Teaching critical thinking skills is one of the greatest challenges facing teachers. More than fifty years ago Benjamin Bloom and his team developed a classification system to organize the various levels of thinking skills (Bloom, 1956/1984). This *taxonomy* identified six tiers in a hierarchy beginning with the lowest levels of thinking: knowledge, comprehension, application, analysis, synthesis, and evaluation. In 1999, Lorin Anderson and David Krathwohl (with Bloom's encouragement) led a team to revise the original taxonomy, update the language, and make it more useful to educators (Anderson & Krathwohl, 2001). This simplified taxonomy is still the most widely used model for the development of higher-level thinking skills.

Tasks and activities that focus on the lowest levels (remembering factual knowledge) may not be as engaging to students as working at the higher levels of thinking (applying, analyzing, synthesizing, creating). The revised taxonomy can help stretch your instructional strategies to more complex learning, which may motivate and interest students.

Norman Webb's Depth of Knowledge

Since the introduction of the Common Core State Standards, another taxonomy has become a popular tool for encouraging higher-level thinking. In 2002, Norman Webb challenged the routine use of Bloom's taxonomy and suggested that it's not about the verb(s)—*applying, synthesizing,* and so forth—it's what comes after. He asked educators, when creating a learning task, to consider what mental processing must occur. In his design of the "Depth of Knowledge" (DOK) taxonomy, he believes that DOK is more about *complexity* than difficulty.

Webb's DOK has merged many of Bloom's taxonomy into four levels of thinking.

1. Recall and Reproduction. Level 1 is the recall of information such as a fact, definition, term, or a simple procedure, as well as performing a simple science process or procedure. This level only requires students to demonstrate a rote response, follow a set procedure or series of steps, or use a well-known formula or algorithm. If the knowledge necessary to answer an item automatically provides the answer to the item, then the item is at Level 1. If the knowledge necessary to answer the item does not automatically provide the answer, the item is at least at Level 2.

Example: Describe the features of a particular location.

2. Skills and Concepts. Level 2 includes the engagement of some mental processing beyond recalling or reproducing a response. The content knowledge involved is more complex than that in Level 1. Students might need to make some decisions as to how to approach the question or problem, and these actions use more than one step. For example, interpreting information from a simple graph or reading information from a graph is at Level 2.

Example: Describe the causes of a historical event.

3. Strategic Thinking. Level 3 requires a higher level of thinking than the previous two levels. It involves reasoning, planning, and using evidence. The cognitive demands at Level 3 are complex and abstract.

This level often involves multistep tasks that require more demanding reasoning. An activity that has more than one possible answer and requires students to justify their responses would most likely be a Level 3 task.

Example: Determine the author's purpose and describe how it affects the interpretation of a reading selection.

4. Extended Thinking. Tasks at Level 4 involve very high cognitive demands and are very complex. At this level, students are required to make several connections and relate ideas within a content area or among several areas. The task always involves selecting or devising many approaches and alternatives for how a situation can be solved. Extended thinking tasks involve research and work to be done *over time.*

Example: Investigate and explain how common themes are found across fables and tales from different cultures.

Understanding the higher levels of the DOK taxonomy may help teachers create challenging and rigorous tasks. Content knowledge is certainly needed to complete the task successfully, but the scope of the learning activity can be enhanced by adding strategic thinking and extended thinking tasks. Many students will find the rigor of the deep learning activities more motivating than the more mundane lower levels of thinking (Aungst, 2014).

> "Our capacity to think is fueled by our storehouses of memory and knowledge acquired by living in complex physical and social worlds. But the ancient feeling states help forge our memories in the first place." (Weintraub, 2012, p. 66)

Creative Thinking

In this tertiary processing level, the SEEKING system is also involved in searching for new ideas and innovations by using imagination, creativity, and synthesis. While higher-level critical thinking involves research, analysis, and evaluation about existing data, creativity involves divergent and convergent thinking skills. To be creative requires generating many unique ideas (divergent thinking) and then combining those ideas into the best result (convergent thinking).

The key is that in the cerebral cortex, we can *play* with ideas and time. We can *imagine* things and ideas that are not in the here and now. In *The Element* (2009), Ken Robinson suggests that our ability to imagine "underpins every uniquely human achievement" (p. 57). You are using your imagination when you can visualize something. Robinson defines imagination as "the power to bring to mind things that are not present to our senses" (p. 58). Not only can we bring to mind things that we have experienced in our past, but we can also hypothesize, conjecture, and synthesize new ideas.

Using our imagination, our ability to time travel in our brain and distort reality to our whims, we can begin to create. Imagination is an *internal* higher level thinking process. When you begin to be creative, you now apply your imagination to manifest an idea, a product, a theory, an art medium, a performance, and so forth. Creativity means you have to *do* something with your imaginative thoughts. It is "the process of having original ideas that have value" (Robinson, 2009, p. 67).

We are born ready to SEEK out new ideas, to imagine, and to create. It is part of our survival need. As the world evolves and expands, we must continually synthesize and create new ideas for how we will survive and thrive in the unknowable future. We also SEEK to experience pleasure, beauty, fun, freedom, and joy. This inner drive becomes our passion that fuels us to create.

Promoting Creativity in School

Have we created an educational system that not only ignores the inner creative drive present in all children, but one that may actually undermine it? Kim (2012) reported that creativity and creative attitudes have steadily declined in the United States since 1990. While general intelligence has continued to grow as expected, the ability to generate unusual ideas and to elaborate on an idea have decreased. Kim refers to this trend as "the Creativity Crisis" and believes that it starts in schools (Bronson & Merryman, 2010). Many young children are not encouraged to seek out new ideas or to generate original thoughts. We seem to be more concerned about every student learning a prescribed, ever-growing curriculum. While we may believe and profess that imagination and creativity are important skills to develop, we allow little freedom within the school day for students to practice the art—let alone SEEK out opportunities to explore and experiment. Kim also believes that another culprit in the decline of creativity is the amount of time children spend with television and technology rather than engaging in creative play. (Note: This is not the same as using technology in a creative way to design, invent, produce, and publish.)

Creativity can be taught, but, more important, a variety of scenarios can be implemented within schools that can promote imaginative thinking and creative production. Not surprisingly, schools that implemented problem-based learning and project-based curriculums demonstrated significant gains in students' overall creativity. Reporters Po Bronson and Ashley Merryman detailed some practical suggestions in their *Newsweek* article titled "The Creativity Crisis."

> Preschool children, on average, ask their parents about 100 questions a day. Why, why, why—sometimes parents just wish it'd stop. Tragically, it does stop. By middle school they've pretty much stopped asking. It's no coincidence that this same time is when student motivation and engagement plummet. They didn't stop asking questions because they lost interest: it's the other way around. They lost interest because they stopped asking questions. (Bronson & Merryman, 2010)

Were you a student who eagerly looked forward to art class? Perhaps you were passionate about creative writing and were motivated when you got to choose your own topic? For Martha, the possibility of creating a skit from a literary passage or creating a diorama of a historic event provided the motivation and excitement to be creative. Coauthor Gayle Gregory was highly motivated by home economics classes that encouraged her to do everything from cooking to fashion design.

Looking forward to opportunities to be creative are strong motivators for capable students as well as reluctant learners.

In the 1970s a classic study was done involving preschoolers and drawing. After three weeks, the children who were given a reward for their work exhibited a decline in their interest and pleasure for drawing. A study conducted more recently by Teresa Amabile of the Harvard Business School demonstrated similar results. She calls her findings the *"Intrinsic Motivation Principle of Creativity*, or the propensity for human creativity to flourish when people are motivated by the personal enjoyment of the work itself"* (McNerney, 2012).

People are most creative when they are motivated by a passionate interest, but Hennessey and Amabile (1987) offer six other *social* criteria that educators may want to consider to foster intrinsic motivation and ultimately imagination and creativity.

- **Evaluation:** The expectation that one's product or creation will be judged can have a negative effect on creativity.
- **Surveillance:** When one is being carefully observed, creativity is diminished and anxiety is raised.
- **Reward:** The quality or type of reward isn't so much of an influence, but it can often undermine the creativity of the outcome if it is expected.
- **Competition:** Young children and adults perform more creatively and accurately when there is no competition; however, research indicated that teens may actually respond to mild competition (Hennessey & Amabile, 1987).
- **Restriction of choice:** A sense of internal control and freedom enhances creativity. Requiring students to follow a certain path or procedure reduces creativity and motivation.
- **Time pressures:** Having sufficient time can increase creativity, and unreasonable deadlines may decrease creativity.

Teaching Creative Thinking Strategies

Explicitly teaching some creative thinking strategies may encourage students' SEEKING systems to engage in creative tasks. Creative thinking is usually open-ended and often a little messy. Thinking creatively demands generating lots of possible answers or ideas. Learning skills to help with brainstorming and looking at problems from different points of view can help build a brain's capabilities. While enthusiastic SEEKING is a natural urge, producing viable creative ideas at the tertiary level can be realized by learning and practicing a few successful creative thinking strategies. It is also important to develop strong self-regulation skills to deal with risk and failure, as well as a growth mindset. Thinking creatively can be highly motivating. Dopamine surges through one's brain as the ideas are flowing.

de Bono's Thinking Tools

Edward de Bono has been the leading authority in the world in the field of creative thinking and is responsible for encouraging the explicit teaching of thinking as a skill in education systems around the world. He created multiple strategies to encourage both critical and creative thinking. He developed the PMI (Plus-Minus-Interesting) tool and originally published it in 1982 in *de Bono's Thinking Course* (de Bono, 1994). Using the PMI thinking tool can help you make decisions quickly by weighing the pros and cons of a decision. It is also helpful for widening your understanding of a problem and for uncovering issues that you might not ordinarily have considered. The PMI strategy is particularly helpful with a group, especially among team members who may strongly favor a particular idea, point of view, or plan. The tool encourages each person to consider other perspectives and can assist in making a well-informed decision.

P-M-I. Determine a proposal or idea that you are considering. Create a graphic organizer with three columns labeled "Plus," "Minus," and "Interesting." In the column underneath "Plus," brainstorm and write down all of the possible positive consequences of taking the action. Underneath "Minus," brainstorm and write down all of the negative effects that might happen. In the "Interesting" column, write down all of the interesting implications (neither good or bad) and possible outcomes of taking the action. Use the lists to generate a discussion that may help students come to a consensus.

Six Thinking Hats. In 1999, de Bono created another creative thinking strategy called Thinking Hats (Lens or Masks). Six Hat thinking helps students examine different perspectives on a topic or issue. Each colored hat represents a different point of view. Using different-colored hats is a great gimmick, but you could use colored magnifying glasses or masks of different colors to vary the process. In a small-group brainstorm, students can assume the point of view of a specific hat assigned to them. As an individual creative thinking task, each student could use flexible thinking to put himself or herself in another's shoes by thinking of an appropriate response based on the attribute of the hat (see Figures 5.3 and 5.4).

Technology as a Motivator for Creativity

While too much time with TV and computer games may decrease intrinsic motivation, educators must embrace how technology might be used to increase motivation and creativity.

> Technology will not live up to its potential until we start to think of it less like televisions and more like paintbrushes. That is, we need to start seeing computer screens not simply as information machines, but also as a new medium for creative design and expression. The more we learn about the abilities of technology, the more creative we become. (Saxena, 2013)

As schools recognize the potential of technology as a creativity generator, they will see that a variety of technological tools can help enhance student motivation. Digital storybooks, infographics, cartooning, blogs, mind-mapping tools, video and auditory production, global communication, and even games can all be utilized to enhance student motivation and creativity. Students must have access to and time with a variety of technology tools to build their skills, confidence, and imagination (Wikipedia, n.d.).

FIGURE 5.3

Six Hat Template

White Hat  Just the facts	• Only the facts! • Details and information	
Purple Hat  Judgment	• Negative issues • Problems • Obstacles	
Red Hat  Feel it!	• Emotions and feelings • Opinions and reactions	
Green Hat  Growth and potential	• Where could this go? • Possibilities • Outgrowths • Seeds of creativity	
Yellow Hat  Optimistic	• What's the upside? • Considering possibilities	
Blue Hat  Cool and collected	• Reflections • Metacognition • Implications	

FIGURE 5.4

Six Hat Sample: The Civil War

White Hat		
 Just the facts	• Only the facts! • Details and information	• What conditions led to the confrontation? • Who was involved? • Who were the heroes? • What were the results?
Purple Hat  Judgment	• Negative issues • Problems • Obstacles	• What was a problem with the notion of civil war? • What were some of the negative effects?
Red Hat  Feel it!	• Emotions and feelings • Opinions and reactions	• How was the Civil War perceived by the North and South?
Green Hat  Growth and potential	• Where could this go? • Possibilities • Outgrowth • Seeds of creativity	• How was the Civil War the beginning of a new culture in the United States?
Yellow Hat  Optimistic	• What's the upside? • Considering possibilities	• What innovations resulted from the Civil War?
Blue Hat  Cool and collected	• Reflections • Metacognition • Implications	• In reflection, how did the Civil War help advance American society? Support your answer with evidence.

Motivating Students with Problems and Projects

What can educators do that will motivate students to think at high levels, develop creativity, and practice 21st century skills? To promote engagement of the SEEKING system at the highest level, the answers are fairly straightforward:

> Traditional academic approaches—those that employ narrow tasks to emphasize rote memorization or the application of simple procedures—won't develop learners who are critical thinkers or effective writers and speakers. Rather, students need to take part in complex, meaningful projects that require sustained engagement and collaboration. (Barron & Darling-Hammond, 2008, p. 1)

When students can work on real-world authentic tasks that involve communicating, researching, analyzing, decision making, producing, and contributing, their motivation is enhanced, creativity is sparked, and engagement is inevitable. Working to solve a problem or collaborating to create a project are two nearly foolproof ways to engage students' brains. Problem-based learning tasks may be modified to fit a class period or an extended period of study. Project-based learning tasks may include a variety of subject areas and multiple tasks within the assignment. Project-based curricula, in general, demand more time. Both of these models have the potential to energize and motivate students and teachers.

Problem-Based Learning: Using Reasoning and Resources to Solve a Problem

> Challenges, especially real-world challenges, invite students to use their imagination to extend thinking about what is known in order to solve real problems. (Drapeau, 2014, p. 60)

What Is It?

Problem-based learning originated at the medical school of McMaster University in Hamilton, Ontario, in the 1960s. It is a student-centered curriculum where students learn about the subject matter by SEEKING what they need to know to solve problems that are presented. Problems are often authentic and complex, and may even be ill structured (with many possible solutions). Problem-based learning helps learners engage in self-directed learning, sourcing flexible knowledge, while fostering problem solving, resource gathering, reasoning, critical thinking, and collaborative skills fueled by intrinsic motivation.

A traditional problem-based task involves students working in small groups, selecting a problem to solve (or question to answer), identifying what they already know, creating a hypothesis, identifying what they need to know, and working through a plan to validate or refute the hypothesis.

Why Do It?

This pedagogy is a form of active (brain-engaged) learning. It taps into the brain's natural SEEKING system and fosters dopamine release as students move toward solving the problem. The brain is naturally curious and collaborative, and this type of problem solving engages both needs.

Gardner's (2004) definition of intelligence is the ability to solve problems, handle crises, and create things of value in society. The ability to problem solve is a lifelong skill and needs multiple practices to be developed. Sternberg (1996) also suggests that people need to go beyond knowing and create things that are practical, analytical, and creative. These problems should have a capacity to engage students in meaningful, real-world problems, issues, hot topics, or debates.

Barron and Darling-Hammond (2008) report that students involved in problem-based learning are better at generating hypotheses, applying knowledge, providing coherent explanations, supporting their claims with evidence, and evaluating their results. All these skills are targeted within the scope of the Common Core State Standards.

Problem-based learning can benefit *all* learners by providing a meaningful, differentiated, and challenging task. Some of the rewards of this approach include the following:

- Authentic, real-world tasks pique students' SEEKING systems and generate motivation.
- Multiple opportunities for collaboration require students to work together to solve problems.
- An interdisciplinary problem can include multiple curricular content areas.
- Challenging tasks within a student's zone of proximal development (Vygotsky, 1978) increases motivation.
- Complex problems can require both critical and creative thinking skills.

How Do We Do It?

The question/problem to be solved may be proposed by the teacher (greater control over the content and learning targets) or generated by the students (lesser control over the content and objectives). The teacher both activates and facilitates the plan through support and offers guidance while monitoring the process.

Three great ways to frame questions that generate thinking and encourage SEEKING entail asking "Why?" "How?" and "Which is best?"

Why? Why do things happen the way they do?

This type of question requires analysis of cause and effect and the relationship between variables. *Examples:* Why would some people want SeaWorld to close? Why have student absences from school been diminished this year? Why is it important to be a blood donor?

How? How could things be made better?

This question is the basis for problem solving and synthesis. *Examples:* How does the president of the United States impact a 5th grade student? How can our community help reduce beach trash? How can the school's quad area be redesigned to improve student relationships?

Which is best? Which do I select?

This type of question requires deep learning through research and then thoughtful decision making based on clear evidence.

Examples: Which type of diet would be best to avoid developing high cholesterol? Which type of car should you choose if "sustainability" were your highest priority?

Here are examples of other good "problems":
- Should the highest volume setting on an iPod be lowered?
- Our class has raised money to help local homeless people. How should we decide to whom we should give it?
- The school board is considering altering the school week to four days. What should our class's recommendation be?
- What would be a safe and more efficient plan for a fire drill at our school?

Although ill-structured problems may provide an opportunity for multiple solutions, they may prove to be quite challenging for younger students. The following criteria will help guide development of good questions or problems. Good questions or problems

- will incorporate the standards and content to be targeted in the curriculum,
- require resourcing and additional information that is given to students,
- have multiple solutions and pathways,
- evolve hypotheses as new information is unearthed,
- generate controversy and interest and additional questions,
- are more than recall as they are open-ended and complex,
- require collaboration necessary to foster critical and creative thinking, and
- encourage examination of authentic subject content.

Steps in the Problem-Solving Process

1. The problem is presented. Teachers may use minilectures to set the context and introduce the problem (Allen, Duch, & Groh, 1996; Gallagher, 1997), or students may identify the problem.

2. Students engage in group discussion to activate prior knowledge.

3. Through collaboration, the group decides on a hypothesis or initial course of action (rather than listening to suggestions from a teacher or following a set of directions).

4. Students gather data and resources.

5. Students plan their inquiry and investigation.

6. Students evaluate outcomes and solutions as a group.

This chart may be useful for students to organize their thinking related to the problem.

Problem: _____

What do we know?	What is our hypothesis?	What do we need to know?	What is our plan?

The Teacher's Role in Problem-Based Learning (PBL)

As students take an active role in their learning by SEEKING solutions to a challenging task, teachers must modify their roles and become facilitators. A teacher's role is to

- guide the group process,
- encourage participation,
- ask more questions,
- insist on "evidence,"
- model good reasoning,
- offer instruction when needed, and
- provide access to resources.

Effect of PBL on Student Learning and Motivation

Students will create strong connections between concepts when they actively engage with information instead of being passive recipients of it (Gallagher, 1997; Resnick & Klopfer, 1989). Students tend to work harder and with more effort and attention than the passivity a lecture elicits. More thinking, both critical and creative, are involved.

Students often find this type of learning satisfying as their dopamine levels are charged. Learners can also see how this instruction is more helpful for real life than "sit and get" would be. PBL helps students learn collaboration and research skills, along with problem-solving and decision-making skills.

> One must reconsider what students really need to learn and the environment in which they learn. Much of the enthusiasm for the problem-based approach to learning comes from instructors who feel revitalized by the creative energy it releases. (White, 1995)

Project-Based Learning

Project-based learning engages students in completing complex tasks that typically result in a realistic product, an event, or a presentation to an audience. When students have opportunities to work on extended complex tasks, they develop much more than factual content knowledge—they also begin to develop a slew of 21st century skills. An effective project-based curriculum aims to take learning one step further by helping students *transfer* their learning to real-world situations. It is easy to see why PBL might be especially attractive to students' SEEKING systems:

Traditional Instructional Design	Project-Based Learning
• Teacher-directed instruction	• Learner centered
• Textbooks	• Real informative texts
• Workbooks—packets of worksheets	• Student-generated tasks as needed
• Frequent tests	• Authentic summative assessment
• Students work independently	• Students work in groups and with partners
• Grades to inform abilities	• Project's success as authentic assessment

When working on a project, students have multiple tasks. They must work together over an extended time to complete the project. Students develop feelings of self-worth, leadership, efficacy, inclusion, and contribution. Social skills such as cooperation, compassion, and impulse control can be practiced when working in a project group. Project-based activities demand that students see how work and perseverance must be maintained for long periods of time.

> To build grit in students, put them in situations that require it. Instead of asking them to show grit by finding ways to sit dutifully through years of meaningless assignments and boring instructional methods, give students challenging, long-term projects that call for grit. (Larmer, 2014)

Many students are attracted to project-based curriculum design. Their motivation is high when provided opportunities to do this type of task. The most powerful projects will incorporate local resources—maybe even local issues. Great projects almost always culminate with a chance to contribute to the community, build something, make a presentation, raise money, change opinions, or help others with a need. All these types of results can generate an urge to continue participation. Our SEEKING systems are designed to gravitate to challenges, contributions, and relevant tasks (Panksepp & Biven, 2012). Any project that can be adapted to the phrase "Think globally, act locally" may inspire a project-based lesson. Here are some other ideas:

• Students define and seek solutions to the expanding homeless population in "A Student's Guide to Ending Homelessness." Students decide what their focus will be: raising awareness, outreach, direct service, or all of the above. Learn more at http://www .mnhomelesscoalition.org/downloads/Students%20Guide%20to %20Ending%20Homelessness.pdf

• The Salmon and Trout Education Project (STEP) selects classrooms in which to set up freshwater aquariums to raise salmon fry, culminating in a release into a local stream. Learn more at http://salmontrouteducationprogram.com/

• The Edible Schoolyard Network connects educators around the world to build and share a K-12 edible education curriculum, plant a school garden to study nutrition and agronomy, and share the bounty with a local food pantry. Learn more at http://edibleschoolyard.org/

• In "My Place in History," students work with local senior citizens to capture and create their biographies. Work continues as students become advocates for senior citizens. Learn more at http://www.marylandpublicschools.org/NR/rdonlyres/AB3A2D5C-7020-46D4-9D96-ADCD0D73EB66/24900/MyPlaceinHistory.pdf

Project-based learning provides wonderful opportunities for students to develop higher cognitive processes. By working on real-world relevant tasks, the cerebral cortex will be drawing on primary and secondary emotional processing systems to make judgments and form opinions. The brain's SEEKING system will be fully engaged and highly motivated to solve problems and produce results. As more successful projects are completed, students will begin to develop self-confidence and self-worth. They are becoming integral contributors to the world.

The growing body of research presented by Barron and Darling-Hammond (2008) on "teaching for meaningful learning" leads to these conclusions:

• Students learn more deeply when they can apply classroom-gathered knowledge to real-world problems and when they take part in projects that require sustained engagement and collaboration.

• Active learning practices have a more significant impact on student performance than any other variable, including student background and prior achievement.

• Students are most successful when they are taught how to learn as well as what to learn. (Barron & Darling-Hammond, 2008, p. 8)

A Nontraditional Curriculum

Sugata Mitra, a well-known educational researcher and professor, postulates that in the 21st century, "knowing is obsolete." As an experiment, Mitra put a computer with Internet access in a "hole in the wall" in the slum area of New Delhi in 1999. He left it there with a hidden camera to videorecord the activity. What Mitra and fellow researchers saw were children playing with the computer, learning how to go online and get information, and then teaching others. Even though they didn't speak or read English, they were able to learn many things—including navigating the technology without any formal training. Their innate curiosity, enthusiastic motivation, and sense of wonder propelled the students to persevere and figure things out. This experiment became Mitra's inspiration for his "School in the Cloud" (Mitra, 2013).

Mitra suggests that students can find and understand new concepts and remember them better if they are given questions and research tools, and then are allowed to explore the Internet (as well as other avenues) to find what they need to know to answer them—even if those resources are not in their native language. He believes that factual knowledge can be accessed easily in today's technological world, but problem solving, decision making, and creativity must be developed through meaningful and interesting opportunities.

Self-Organized Learning Environment

Mitra also contends that learning can be a self-organized system. The Self-Organized Learning Environment (SOLE) evolved from the School in the Cloud. It is a place where students can work in groups, access the Internet and other software, follow up on a class activity or project, or go where their interests lead them. Allowing students to generate questions relating to a topic and providing time to pursue answers is launching the SEEKING system at any age or grade level.

Anyone can create a Self-Organized Learning Environment (SOLE)—to spark curiosity in children by asking them to explore a "big" question using the Internet and their ability to work together. Learning happens spontaneously in these purposefully chaotic environments. (Mitra on the School in the Cloud website, www.theschoolinthecloud.org)

The Wikihow website takes you through the SOLE process step-by-step (www.wikihow.com/Set-Up-a-Self-Organized-Learning -Environment-%28SOLE%29-at-School).

The teacher's role is to

1. set the stage,
2. make space for SOLE,
3. plan for SOLE and establish patterns for working,
4. initiate the first SOLE experience,
5. troubleshoot, and
6. plan future SOLE activities.

Tertiary processing of the SEEKING system develops our ability to begin to think beyond the present, imagine, create, synthesize, and make cognitively sophisticated plans (Wright & Panksepp, 2012). By providing opportunities for students to work on meaningful, relevant problems and projects, educators can help develop and apply these higher cognitive processes. Now the learner searches for new ideas and systems, and creates innovations by using imagination, creativity, and synthesis.

Part III

Bringing It
All Together:

Engaging the SEEKING System

6

Leveraging the SEEKING System to Maximize Student Attention, Engagement, and Perseverance

Creating a Brain-Friendly, SEEKING-Friendly Classroom

Safe and Secure Environments

Creating the climate and environment conducive for learning is imperative for intrinsic motivation and allowing the SEEKING system to be activated. As previously stated, brains have to be safe in order to be fully engaged and to avoid reverting to the fight, flight, or freeze mode. Students need to feel that they have unconditional regard and are respected and that the teacher and fellow students support them. Predictable routines and conditions help provide that safety. A brain-friendly classroom has conditions that students can count on to meet their basic needs.

Collaboration

Students also need to engage in safe social collaboration. Providing daily opportunities for students to use dialogue more than they experience monologue is mandatory. Building community inclusion is critical, along with norms of how students work together. Social skills must be taught so that they have effective practices to work together successfully and productively. Learning to listen attentively, respect others' ideas, and consider different viewpoints are key skills for success in groups.

To activate high-quality group work in your classroom:

1. **Communicate instructional objectives:** determine group size, group formation, room arrangements, materials, and student roles.

2. **Orchestrate the academic task:** explain the task and structure positive interdependence, accountability, criteria for success, and desired behaviors.

3. **Observe and intervene:** monitor and provide assistance, question, prompt, and help resolve any conflict that may arise.

4. **Evaluate and process:** provide closure, assess and evaluate student learning, and provide opportunities for group processing and celebration.

Firsthand Experiences

Doing the "real thing" is always more engaging than just hearing or reading about it. The Chinese proverb reminds us "I hear and I forget; I see and I remember; I do and I understand."

Concrete materials and manipulatives are helpful in creating a real experience and developing a concrete understanding before moving to abstract thinking. Although field trips are rapidly disappearing due to financial constraints, virtual (digital) opportunities can transport students to appropriate topics and locations. In addition, artifacts related to the topics being studied always intrigue learners.

Choice and Self-Directedness

Choice is empowering and engaging. The notion of a sense of control is equally as motivating. Innate in most learners, self-directed learning encompasses both of these critical elements of a brain-friendly classroom. "In its broadest meaning, 'self-directed learning' describes a process by which individuals take the initiative, with or without the assistance of others, in diagnosing their learning needs, formulating learning goals, identifying human and material resources for learning, choosing and implementing appropriate learning strategies, and evaluating learning outcomes" (Knowles, 1975, p. 18). In self-directed learning:

- Students take more responsibility for their learning.
- Students do not learn in isolation.
- The transfer of learning to other issues increases.
- Learning may occur in groups, alone, via digital activities, or with a variety of other resources.
- The teacher's role shifts to guide, resource provider, assessor, and questioner.

Dopamine release is part of the reason that self-directed learning is so engaging. It is the predictive power of success that causes the learner to focus attention and release dopamine. If the experience is new and novel, the learner is able to focus more completely. The dopamine release also helps in memory processing: we remember the experience and learning in a positive way. Both episodic (experience) and semantic (factual) memories are enhanced.

Self-directed learning allows the student to direct what and how he or she will learn to become proficient with the standard targeted. The autonomy of choice is motivating and empowering. Making a choice elicits a commitment to the task. It's hard to say "I won't do this" or "I can't" when the student has chosen it.

Keeping Students in "Flow"

Psychologist Mihaly Csikszentmihalyi suggests that flow is what makes life worth living (Csikszentmihalyi, 1988; Csikszentmihalyi, Abuhamde, & Nakamura, 2005). It is the "root of happiness." Flow is the mental state that is achieved when a person performing an activity is immersed in a feeling of energized focus, full involvement, and enjoyment in the process of the activity. Don't teachers want that for all our students during the school day?

Nakamura and Csikszentmihalyi (2001) identify six factors that characterize an experience of flow:

- Intense and focused concentration
- Quick action and awareness
- A loss of self-consciousness
- A feeling of personal control over the situation or activity
- Being oblivious to the passage or concept of time
- Experiencing the task as intrinsically rewarding

Flow theory emphasizes three conditions that must be met to achieve a flow state:

- The activity has a clear set of goals and progress offering structure to the task.
- The task must have clear and immediate feedback to allow one to adjust performance to maintain the state of flow.
- One must have a good balance between the *perceived* challenges of the task at hand and one's own *perceived* skills. One must have confidence in one's ability to complete the task at hand.

Schaffer (2013) proposes seven flow conditions:

- Knowing what to do
- Knowing how to do it
- Knowing how well you are doing
- Knowing where to go next
- High perceived challenges
- High perceived skills
- Freedom from distractions

Schaffer also published the Flow Condition Questionnaire to measure each of these seven flow conditions for any given task or activity.

Group Flow

Csikszentmihalyi suggests several ways a group can work together so that each individual member achieves flow. These ideas also help students develop collaborative skills while focusing on problem solving and creativity. The characteristics of such a group include

- creative spatial arrangements,

- norms established to guide group interaction,
- organized working,
- clear expectations understood by all,
- using differences among participants as an opportunity, rather than an obstacle, and
- welcoming complementary ideas and skills.

Flow and Games

Flow is one of the main reasons that people play video games. The primary goal of games is to create entertainment through intrinsic motivation, which is related to flow. Through the balance of skill and challenge, the player's brain is aroused, with attention engaged and motivation high (Rutledge, 2012). Thus, the use of flow in games helps foster an enjoyable experience that in turn increases motivation and draws players to continue playing. As such, game designers strive to integrate flow principles into their projects (Chen, 2008). Overall, the experience of play is fluid and intrinsically psychologically rewarding independent of scores or in-game successes in the flow state.

Teachers can use games to introduce material, increase retention, and improve understanding. Feedback is a necessary component, and repetition and practice are required for memory. Students don't learn complex tasks in one exposure. Specific feedback is key to developing competency, which is evident in games where players perform just beyond their peak and are guided by clear goals and feedback (Rutledge, 2012). The positive emotions associated with flow are related to the law of effect, which suggests that learning is strengthened with positive feelings and pleasant conditions and when the task is relevant and meaningful for the learner.

Ways to Help Students Get in Flow

Vygotsky's Social Development Theory

How do we create conditions and experiences that foster flow? Psychologist Lev Vygotsky's social development theory may be helpful in this regard. This theory has three major components. The first is that social interaction plays a vital role in learning and cognition. Learners need multiple interactions with teachers and peers to help deepen understanding. It is necessary to create positive relationships with teachers and peers in an environment that is emotionally, cognitively, and physically supportive, free of threat or punishment, and where trial and error is encouraged. These interactions are enhanced through "more knowledgeable others" (MKOs), whether peers or teachers. Interactions, with a variety of resources, including technology are part of the process.

The second component of social development theory is that learners are clear about the goals and relevancy of the tasks. Expectations and criteria are important if students are to achieve flow. As Stiggins (1993b) often pointed out, usually one can hit a target if it is clear and holds still long enough.

The third component is Vygotsky's notion of the zone of proximal development (ZPD). Not only is the MKO necessary, but also the task must be within reach. Students are bored if the task is not challenging or frustrated if it is unlikely that they can be successful. So it makes sense to balance the level of complexity and challenge of tasks with the skill level of students. This approach requires pre-assessment to evaluate the student's prior knowledge or exposure to the lesson's content, concepts, or skills. This information is essential so that teachers can better challenge at the appropriate level of "stretch."

To foster flow, we also need to tap into the motivational drives (e.g., support of the learner's sense of autonomy or perceived competency). Encouraging students to make choices in tasks based on extending their learning and praising effort and progress rather than "smartness" will also increase motivation.

Classroom Environment

Environmental support, as well as environmental challenge, are both necessary for the flow experience. It won't help to give challenging tasks if the support is not available. Without it, anxiety will be experienced instead of flow.

Environmental support is conveyed by constructive feedback. Offering constructive feedback in a timely fashion is key to facilitating flow and providing opportunities to be both active and interactive.

Adolescent students report high engagement when referring to many after-school programs, even school-based programs. Students can also be highly engaged in art, academic, and athletic programs.

As teachers, we need to design environments and tasks with more personal relevancy, relationships, and appropriate demands to developmental needs. The mere management of students in the industrial model is not an environment that provides engagement for the culturally and cognitively diverse students we now serve.

Discovering Each Student's Sweet Spot

When students are at a crystallizing moment of learning, they experience a point where attention, high interest, positive feelings, and a connection to prior successes collide. This is informally referred to as the "sweet spot"—that place where a combination of factors results in a maximum response for a given amount of effort.

The Learner's Sweet Spot

Attention
- Novelty
- Survival
- Learning preferences
- Basic needs
- Pattern detection

Interest
- Meaningful
- Relevancy
- Prior knowledge
- Pre-assessment

Positive Feelings
- Safe and secure environment
- Laughter, joy, humor
- Culturally sensitive

Prior Successes
- Growth mindset
- Choices
- Process and products

Source: Adapted from *Think Big, Start Small* (Gregory & Kaufeldt, 2012).

Skillful teachers seek the sweet spot for learning in their students by surveying prior knowledge or experience, identifying what created prior success for them, and predicting what degree of interest they might have in the task. As we examine the four components important to create the sweet spot, consider the following:

Positive Feelings (Emotions)

- Is there a safe and secure emotional climate and environment?
- Do students feel included?
- Is the classroom culturally responsive?

Attention and Engagement

- What will activate the SEEKING system: novelty, humor, movement?
- Are the learners' basic needs being met?
- Are learner preferences considered?
- What is the students' prior knowledge and readiness?

Interest

- What is the "hook" for learners?
- What pre-assessment tools will access prior knowledge?
- How will relevance and meaning be addressed?

Prior Successes

- What types of tasks have elicited student engagement and success?
- Are choices and options for student selection available?

Learners do better when the climate is supportive and responsive to their needs and when their preferences and strengths are tapped. If we try to focus on our students' sweet spots and take into account their affective, cognitive, physiological, and psychological needs, they will feel respected and comfortable, be able to take risks, and persevere to be successful.

Being Culturally Responsive

Racial, ethnic, and linguistic demographics have changed dramatically since 1972, when only 22 percent of students in the United States had minority backgrounds. By 2003, that number had increased to 41 percent of enrollment in elementary and secondary schools. As of 2006, one in five students speaks a language other than English at home and are learning English in school (Center on Education Policy, 2006).

This diversity in our classrooms requires not only special teaching skills but also a new mindset for teachers, who need to understand the role of language and culture in learning (Villegas & Lucas, 2002). Several issues need to be addressed in order to provide effective opportunities for diverse students.

Understanding How Learners Make Meaning

We know that prior knowledge is key to new learning. However, minority groups may be lacking in prior knowledge and need "bridges" or "back-filling" to be receptive and confident and not in a fight, flight, or freeze mode. Honoring their journey and their families will have them SEEKING to feel good about their challenges. Helping the whole family assimilate into the community will make them feel that their culture is valued and valuable in their learning.

Learning About Students' Lives

Just as we hope teachers do with all students, we need to get to know about these new citizens. The more we learn about their culture and social groups, family makeup, favorite activities, strengths, and concerns, the more empathy we have for our students. This might include home visits, attending cultural social events, having discussions about their aspirations, and finding ways for them to share their culture with classmates. Many teachers may not be a part of the minority groups they serve and have lives that differ from these immigrant families. It is imperative that teachers have sociocultural consciousness and hold affirming attitudes toward diversity (Nieto, 1996).

This attitude greatly influences the student–teacher and peer relationships that are so important for brain-friendly environments.

Becoming Socioculturally Conscious

Sociocultural consciousness is one's awareness that people's worldviews vary based on life experiences and factors such as ethnicity, race, gender, and social class. If we as educators only rely on our own personal experiences, we may not be as sensitive to others as we need to be. We may make incorrect assumptions about circumstances or issues about which we have neither experience nor understanding. With the help of professional development and discussions in professional learning communities, teachers can better understand the challenges of minority groups and unearth successful strategies and programs for diverse learning.

Views About Diversity

Research shows that many educators have a deficit perspective when it comes to minority groups (Nieto, 1996). If teachers do not believe students have potential, the students are marginalized in their learning. Teachers may more frequently use outdated "drill and kill" approaches with diverse students as they have low academic expectations regarding their success. They may also ask fewer questions and may not provide sufficient wait time for a minority student to access information and respond.

A teacher's mindset related to the potential of socially subordinated groups can be "fixed." As Dweck (2006) reminds us, a teacher with a growth mindset is more positive in her or his approach to all students. The more we see diverse learners in an affirming way, respect cultural differences, and view them as capable, the more they will rise to the occasion. Teachers assume that they can and will learn, and thus these students develop self-confidence and achieve. Offering interesting, real-world, stimulating, and purposeful instruction will both appeal to learners and increase students' engagement and success.

Applying Appropriate Instructional Strategies

Teachers in any learning situation need to access prior knowledge, and, as noted, doing so is especially important for English language learners and minorities.

Using resources in these students' first language to build background knowledge can serve as a bridge to content knowledge. Cultural novels and narratives can appeal and offer respect for their background. Other appropriate resources, such as study guides and bilingual dictionaries, are helpful. Evidence- and research-based strategies such as using graphic organizers, visuals, and hands-on activities help with vocabulary and concept development. Using analogies from students' cultures may help with constructing new knowledge and understanding in English.

Advocating for Students

Teachers know that they may need different resources for students of different backgrounds. We also know that experienced capable teachers recognize that "fair isn't always equal and equal isn't always fair." Marginalized students may need more time, different texts, different techniques of instruction, experienced teachers, smaller classes, sensitivity to cultural issues, and a curriculum that respects all learners. Helping all learners succeed is part of the conversation in professional learning communities that collectively focus on sharing strategies for student success.

Keeping Dopamine Levels Up

Dopamine is also sometimes referred to as the "save button" in the brain. It is released when the SEEKING system is activated. It has been said that it is the "reward" neurotransmitter, but Panksepp affirms that it is the SEEKING that releases the chemical, not the reward. It is the excitement of the "hunt." The quest is to find. When these conditions are present, the dopamine release acts as appetitive to the task, keeping us focused and attentive and enacting the save button so that we remember easily that which took place (episodic memory). It also ensures that we will pay attention if we encounter this task or something like it again in the future.

As teachers, we know how important attention is to learning and we strive to make learning exciting, novel, relevant, and intriguing to learners. Reinforcement with positive regard is also a way to increase dopamine release.

This again relates to classroom climate and a safe learning community that lowers stress and does not block the flow of incoming data to the neocortex. Classrooms should be

- personally meaningful;
- engaging;
- appropriate developmentally;
- differentiated to accommodate Flow and ZPD;
- appropriate in terms of a level of stress that keeps the pathways

to the neocortex open and does not activate the protective, sensitive amygdala.

Teachers are using brain-friendly strategies that increase the release of dopamine when they employ humor, storytelling, optimism, positive collaboration, choice, and movement. Role playing, drawing and other visual representations, a choice of assessment tools, and cooperative group learning all increase positivity.

When we plan for learning, we are cognizant of the importance of new methods, resources, and processes to captivate the students' attention. The creativity of teachers can meet the challenge of developing the SEEKING system in our students. To keep dopamine levels high for students, we need to help students activate their SEEKING systems with new, exciting, enjoyable, and intriguing adventures in the classroom. Come up with new ways of presenting material, make the experience interesting, and share positive encouraging feedback for effort as well as success. Not only is dopamine released, but the pleasure of the experience also increases another neurotransmitter, acetylcholine, which fosters memory, alertness, and the executive function of the prefrontal cortex.

We need to provide activities that include interaction with peers, laughter, physical movement, listening to music, storytelling, and kindness in a supportive climate to increase dopamine levels. We also support dopamine release when students experience the pride of success in accomplishment and reflect on their abilities and skill set.

Play and Movement to Increase Dopamine

If we know that dopamine is the key neurotransmitter to stimulate the SEEKING system, students might benefit from regular opportunities to increase the amount of dopamine in their brains. Without sufficient *natural* dopamine release, our brains are less motivated, sluggish, and often uninterested. Diet and nutrition can help improve levels of dopamine, but for a "quick fix," movement and exercise are the way to go in school settings.

When we sit too long, blood pools in our lower extremities, and oxygen and glucose are depleted in the brain. Movement helps pump blood to the brain. It lowers cortisol and saline in the blood and increases dopamine. Asking students to move into groups, stand and talk with a partner, distribute supplies, or give a standing ovation to a presentation are ways of moving within classtime.

Longer sessions of 20 to 30 minutes of mild exercise increase blood calcium, which in turn stimulates dopamine release. Ratey (2008) states that exercise increases the release of not only dopamine, but also norepinephrine and serotonin—all important neurotransmitters that control our energy, thoughts, and emotions. An added benefit is that with regular stimulation of dopamine release, our brains begin to become better at regulating the tonic levels of dopamine (Ratey, 2008). This can be particularly helpful for students who exhibit attention difficulties.

Even short opportunities to play can increase the brain's dopamine production. Playing a game, engaging in a mild competition, and having a little fun can help the brain get ready for more serious learning activities. Integrating more recess or *free play* as well as orchestrating organized games can change students' brain chemistry and promote motivation and the SEEKING system to engage in learning (Brown, 2009).

Laughter and Music

Another trigger for dopamine release and feeling good is music. Neuroscientist Robert Zatorre (2013) found a dopamine release is triggered in both the dorsal and ventral striatium by music. These areas are associated with responses to pleasurable stimuli. Teachers who incorporate music into the classroom environment stimulate dopamine release. Music causes emotional arousal, raising our pulse and blood pressure, activating the cerebellum (body movements), and sending blood to our legs—perhaps for toe tapping.

Do-Overs

We don't all learn in the same way on the same day. Just as we have to practice sports skills or music techniques, we often have to practice cognitive skills multiple times as well. With feedback and coaching, we all get better over time. We don't want students to have incorrect concepts or deficits going forward, so it is worth the time to reteach and continue to develop concepts and skills that are important to know. Do-overs allow the brain to reprogram and strengthen the correct neural connections. Remember, neurons that fire together, wire together. They also help create patterns or mental schema to create strong memories.

Learning relies on experiences. So if learning doesn't happen with the first exposure, try another one. With do-overs, students can

- examine multiple results;
- identify similarities and differences;
- notice patterns;
- reflect on "aha's" or anomalies;
- create, test, and modify hypotheses; and
- develop schemata such as templates and programs for future use.

Classrooms need to be "brain-safe." Some ways to achieve this environment and climate is to develop norms for safe thinking, which includes making mistakes. Harmin and Toth (2006) suggest trust statements be developed with students so that they can feel safe and also monitor these norms. Here are some examples:

- All opinions count.
- No sarcasm or put-downs allowed.
- Everyone has a voice and can be heard.
- Mistakes help us learn.
- There are no dumb questions.

The reaction to negative feedback varies with age. Children who are 8 or 9 react strongly to positive feedback and not so much to negative (Crone et al., 2006). They are still at a stage of SEEKING and exploration as they try to figure out their environment. With young adolescents, the dopamine/pleasure reward center in the nucleus accumbens increases its reactivity to negative feedback, resulting in huge emotional shifts, but moderates to less extreme shifts in the adult years (Philpot, McQuown, & Kirstein, 2001). This brain development accounts for the sensitivity to negative experiences and mistake recognition in middle and high school and the fact that negative feedback has a more powerful effect than positive feedback with these students.

The fear of making a mistake publicly in class is intense, but we know mistakes help us learn. Critical thinking is necessary to weigh errors and information and to form and strengthen memory pathways. Teachers can aid this process through accurate and immediate corrective feedback. This feedback does not have to be teacher generated. Peer review and the use of rubrics with criteria help students self-correct or adjust their progress toward a goal. The brain is motivated to retain and invest in correct responses that cause dopamine release and pleasurable feelings and to correct errors to minimize a drop in dopamine release. If students are fearful of making errors, they don't participate to the same extent and can't construct new knowledge.

A great resource to help students realize the value of mistakes is *Mistakes That Worked: 40 Inventions and How They Came to Be* (Jones, 1994). This book chronicles inventions we couldn't do without that were discovered through errors, reinforcing the fact that we have to try, fail, and try again to create things of value. It also cautions against quick negative responses to ideas and suggestions, because they might be the seeds of new and unique developments.

About 85 percent of the questions asked in classrooms are asked by the teacher, and for most of them, there is one "right" answer. Students are often playing "trivia pursuit" looking for that single answer. If we truly want to create a brain-friendly environment, we can pose questions and respond to students' answers in ways that make students feel less stress and be more engaged in thinking.

• Ensure that questions are clear and well worded.

• Ask more open-ended questions that require more diverse thinking.

• Use levels of thinking that tap into more than factual recall.

• Reiterate that open-ended questions do not have only one right answer but many possibilities.

• Socratic questioning allows students to offer opinions and creative ideas that can be supported by their ideas or evidence.

• Give students a chance to discuss their responses with others to refine, clarify, and enhance their thinking before large group discussion. Try think-pair-share (Lyman & McTighe, 1988).

• Responses—whether by the teacher or other students—to offered answers should be nonjudgmental and accepting but not qualifying. Try comments like these:

+ Interesting . . .
+ I never thought of that.
+ Can someone add to this thinking?
+ Anything different out there?
+ Maybe . . .

> + Possibly . . .
> + Can you add to that?

Value of Competitions

Students play games all the time on a variety of devices. They can't do this in school. Why would we negate the very thing they choose and enjoy doing? Sixty studies show that using academic games can lead to a 20 percent increase in student achievement (Marzano, 2010). Quite a compelling statistic!

Teachers can use game-show formats such as *Jeopardy!* and *Wheel of Fortune* to infuse content questions with a fun way to rehearse and remember ideas. Mild competition like this taps into the learner's SEEKING system and is engaging for most students.

To get the most out of games, Marzano (2010) offers these suggestions:

• **Provide inconsequential rewards.** Working in teams, students compete for points. The team with the most points gets coupons for the class store which has pens, pencils, stickers, and other trivial items. Teams are restructured regularly so there is a heterogeneous mix with an equal opportunity to get involved and be successful.

• **Target essential content.** These games will only be a help to student learning if they focus on the material that is related to standards and not just fun activities.

• **Debrief the activity.** After the game, have students discuss which questions were difficult, what they didn't understand, and where they needed additional clarification.

• **Make revisions.** Students should review their notes and diagrams and add new ideas or corrections after the game.

Technology

School and the real world are not very much alike. Technology occupies much of students' time, all day long. Unlimited resources, ideas, and social networks all around the world are available to help them collaborate and learn together. Students have choice and limitless options. Real-world technology is more colorful, stimulating, and instantaneous than the average classroom. School for the most part is still the teacher talking and students listening. Students would rather do projects, examine case studies, work in groups, and share information. They want to make a difference in their world (Prensky, 2010).

In Jared Covili's *Going Google* (2012), we learn that 89 percent of young adults are online; 12- to 14-year-olds watch screens about 4.5 hours a day, whether smartphones, tablets, e-readers, computers, TVs, or other video media; and 82 percent of 7th to 12th graders "media multitask" while doing homework. Yet classrooms haven't changed that much, and most of students' personal technology is prohibited from use in the classroom. Even the technology we have available is not used creatively; often blackboards are just replaced with interactive whiteboards. No wonder students use the "*b*-word" to describe school—boring! At one time an outrage erupted in schools when students dared to bring ballpoint pens to school. Imagine! Why do we fight for the status quo?

Technology is instrumental in helping students develop the 21st century skills of collaboration, creativity and innovation, critical thinking, and problem solving. Collaborative projects such as SOLE (Chapter 5) are exciting opportunities for students to use technology. Google is an endless resource to organize and supply information and is available free to the user. Questions can be answered and information tapped at one's fingertips. We need to use technology to foster creativity and innovation and allow students to explore and create without risk. Standards and skills will be learned and retained better through self-discovery and use.

New technologies are developing monthly, and teachers need to allow students to keep up with the times and even let them take the lead. They are eager to do so. The curriculum today must take into account the technology we have available. The use of webcasts, video creation, YouTube, Twitter, blogging, Facebook, and Google are highly motivating to the SEEKING system. These also are great for incorporating all levels of thinking, and they encourage creativity and critical thinking. Students who may not be excited to read a book or listen to a lecture are naturally drawn to media, tackling challenging concepts using PowerPoint, film, or video.

Students don't get the same thrill of handing in a project to a teacher as they do from demonstrating their originality on the Internet to friends, family, and strangers. They get feedback from everywhere. We need to let go of some control and let students create and build success for their futures in the global marketplace.

Promoting Growth Mindsets: The Language of Feedback

As teachers, we can start with ourselves and change our mindset from "fixed" to "growth" as we view our students. The concept of the growth mindset (Dweck, 2006) is also helpful as a reminder to students that they are not yet proficient but can get there with effort and adjustment. When students are reminded that they can develop new skills and concepts over time with effort and rehearsal (just as we would a sports or performance technique), they continue to strive and SEEK and get that motivational dopamine release.

Dweck (2006) noted that in a New York experiment, teachers told one group of students "My, you are really smart" and another group, "You really worked hard on that." What they found was that those students praised for intelligence actually chose less challenging test items the next time to ensure they wouldn't lose their status of "smartness." These students were more likely to give up when tasks were difficult or challenging. In our classrooms, these are the students who give up when things don't come easily. "I can't" is often their response. They believe if you are smart, things should come naturally to you; they don't persist because they believe that they are "dumb" if it takes too much effort. They don't handle setbacks well and may become defensive, blame others, or cheat instead of opting for problem-solving alternatives that might work.

In the experiment Dweck described, those who were praised for effort enjoyed the dopamine rush from the effort and actually tackled more challenging tasks the next time. These are the students who develop a growth mindset and learn to persevere in spite of obstacles. They are resilient and "gritty."

Strategies to increase the notion of a growth mindset in students include praising effort rather than focusing only on success. As mentioned previously, it is imperative that students are more comfortable making a mistake, realizing that it is sometimes through errors that we illuminate the wrong way to do something, reflect, and progress toward competence.

Strategies to Foster a Growth Mindset in the Classroom

The following strategies not only help in the short term but also promote a love of learning for a lifetime.

• Teach students about neuroplasticity and how our brains grow and change with practice and effort. All brains have potential. People have different interests and talents, but we can all learn.

• Share challenges that you had and obstacles you have overcome with effort. Relate stories of people of greatness and the years of practice and coaching it took to be successful.

• Offer appropriate challenges and scaffold steps with resources, prompts, and encouragement. Be there to help strategize, question, suggest, and encourage like a coach. Here are some examples of statements to encourage effort:

> + I know you spent a lot of time on that. It will be worth it.
> + Your effort really produced results.
> + It may seem like hard work, but you are really coming along.
> + With all the effort you are giving, you'll soon be there.
> + You really stuck to it. Good for you!
> + Slow and steady wins the race! You're coming along.

+ I'm happy that you're so dedicated. Good learners
  do that.
+ You seem to be working really hard to figure that out.
+ You've really been trying. Is there anything I can do
  to help?
+ What might you try next?
+ Did you know the geniuses have to work hard?
+ Wow, you chose some good strategies that will
  probably help.

Help students choose a reasonable goal and a plan to achieve it. A timeline and a list of resources (material, human, technology) may be useful. Chronicle progress in a journal to show that they are moving forward toward the goal. Also have them reflect in journal entries on feelings they had as they persisted and made incremental gains, as well as their feelings when they were finally successful.

Parents also need to know about the growth mindset, so share your findings with them at parent-teacher conferences. Explain that praise for intelligence may be doing more harm than good. According to a survey at Columbia University, 85 percent of parents praised their children for being smart, thinking they were helping with self-esteem. However, they may be undermining their children's intelligence growth. Instead of praise for merely existing, parents are wiser to praise effort and persistence when children are persevering at a task, so that they will develop a growth mindset and be ready to accept challenges in their lives.

Teachers' Passion and Enthusiasm

One of the most motivating and supportive elements in the classroom is the teacher's attitude toward students. Another strong motivator is the teacher's enthusiasm for the subject and learning. You can't expect students to be interested, curious, and excited about the lesson if the teacher isn't. In the *Visible Learning* research, Hattie (2009) suggests that teacher/student relationships have a strong impact on student learning.

Students need to know that those who are teaching and learning with them value and respect them as individuals. Everything we do as educators is a message to students revealing our beliefs and values about them personally and academically. The brain is a parallel processor. It takes in all sensory information available to it. It is not just what the teacher says but the tone of voice, body language, and facial expressions. Students, rightly or wrongly, form a mindset of what a teacher thinks or feels about them. If a positive message, this perspective can be a huge motivator for a student that fosters optimism and encourages effort; but if negative, it can be a huge detriment to enhancing their self-esteem and learning potential. Possibility thinking is a real plus in terms of helping learners persist with effort to achieve success.

In a seven-year study conducted with 400 elementary schools, Bryk and Schneider (2002) found that the greater trust that existed between and among all members of the school community (teachers, parents, students, administrators), the higher the results on standardized tests. They coined the idea of "relational trust" to describe the optimal interpersonal social interactions that take place in the school and classroom. Four criteria were identified to develop relational trust:

- *Competence* in the abilities required for the role
- *Respect* for the role that each plays
- *Integrity* for trusting in what people say and do
- *Personal regard* for the efforts and caring of another person

Final Thoughts

Brains don't like being bored. In today's fast-paced digital world, students often see school as very much an unstimulating entity. For the most part, teachers and parents see school as the traditional teacher-led, top-down, "listen to me" place that they experienced growing up. School is probably the least responsive evolving institution in today's society, clinging to the factory model instead of the thinking model.

The dogmas of the quiet past, are inadequate to the stormy present. The occasion is piled high with difficulty, and we must rise—with the occasion. As our case is new, so we must think anew, and act anew. We must disenthrall ourselves, and then we shall save our country.

(Abraham Lincoln, "Annual Message to Congress," December 1, 1862)

If we internalize the message of Lincoln from the perspective of 21st century educators, we must "think anew and act anew."

Brains were made to SEEK, not "sit and get." The digital natives coming into our classrooms today are used to SEEKING, yet we expect them to be in "receive mode" when they enter school. We often push conformity and uniformity rather than unique, creative thinking. Asking to memorize and regurgitate knowledge and facts is not only boring to brains, but also a waste of time given that we can often access that information with a click of the mouse. We really need to teach less so that more learning can take place. Yet, there is a misconception that the more teachers are in monologue mode, the more they are doing their job.

The question is, "What changes in the environment can facilitate that choice such that self-discipline becomes less important?" Perhaps the broader message for educators is this: Focus less on "fixing the kids" and more on improving what and how they're taught. (Kohn, 2014b, p. 25)

Brain-wise, it makes more sense to allow students to direct and construct their own understanding through inquiry, mastering fewer topics more deeply with multiple thinking skills embedded in the process. Have students predict, generate hypotheses, and make relevant connections; then create interesting authentic tasks that build curiosity, access prior knowledge, and build new knowledge.

Students come with adaptive neurons that lead to behavioral and cognitive flexibility resulting from neuroplasticity. Animal research tells us prefrontal cortex neurons in regions of executive function networks rewire connections triggered by new challenges (Storm & Tecott, 2005). Students who arrive at answers that they have unearthed through interactive learning receive a dopamine release during the SEEKING and also commit the learning to long-term memory for future access. Through this process, students learn that there are multiple perspectives to a project or problem, as well as multiple solutions. Their interaction with peers broadens their understanding, and focused dialogue strengthens their vocabulary and concepts relevant to the topic.

Sternberg's *Successful Intelligence* (1996) reminds us that society doesn't only value strictly factual information, except on *Jeopardy!* and other quiz shows. What society wants and deems as "successful intelligence" is people who can do something with what they know: they can be analytical, practical, and creative with knowledge and skills. Given that most knowledge is now a click away, isn't it more logical and productive as a society to activate the SEEKING system—the brain's natural motivator—and have students engage in tasks that move knowledge and skill to the analytical, practical, and creative levels based on input from the learners themselves?

Given what we know about the SEEKING system's potential in the human brain, educators have a natural ally in their quest to motivate and engage learners. Students' brains are programed to "seek and find," and teachers can enhance this need by planning strategically to engage the SEEKING system. Offering novelty and choice intrigues and empowers students. Creating opportunities to investigate, research, solve problems, deal with discrepant events, and search the Internet are key to this engagement. Teachers can help students develop a can-do attitude and a growth mindset by providing tasks at various levels of complexity and challenge, enhance with feedback, and create the conditions for flow (Gregory & Kaufeldt, 2012). In addition, brain-safe classrooms—where students can risk through trial and error, where their dignity is preserved and they feel part of a positive learning community—are essential to manage the stress response system so that brains are focused on learning, not self-preservation. Students are also motivated by the enthusiasm and excitement present in the classroom. Thus, the teacher's passion for learning has a high impact on student motivation and engagement.

> *I agree that this system, so important for generating feelings of "enthusiasm" as opposed to rewarding "pleasure," needs to be on the radar of educators. If this system can be captivated by teachers, they have done half their job.*
> —Jaak Panksepp, personal communication, March 22, 2014

References

Allen, D. E., Duch, B. J., & Groh, S. E. (1996). The power of problem-based learning in teaching introductory science courses. In L. Wilkerson & W. H. Gijselaers (Eds.), *Bringing problem-based learning to higher education: Theory and practice* (pp. 43–52). San Francisco: Jossey-Bass.

Amabile, T. (1987). The motivation to be creative. In S. Isaksen (Ed.), *Frontiers of creativity research: Beyond the basics* (pp. 223–254). Buffalo, NY: Bearly.

Anderson, L., & Krathwohl, D. (Eds.). (2001). *A taxonomy for learning, teaching, and assessing: A revision of Bloom's taxonomy of educational objectives.* New York: Addison, Wesley Longman.

Aronson, J., & Steele, C. M. (2005). Stereotypes and the fragility of human competence, motivation, and self-concept. In C. Dweck & E. Elliot (Eds.), *Handbook of competence & motivation.* New York: Guilford.

Aungst, G. (2014, September 4). Using Webb's Depth of Knowledge to increase rigor. *Edutopia* blog. Available: www.edutopia.org/blog/webbs-depth-knowledge-increase-rigor-gerald-aungst

Baddeley, A. D. (1996). *Your memory: A user's guide* (3rd ed.) London: Prion Books.

Baddeley, A. D. (1997). *Human memory: Theory and practice (rev. ed).* Hove, United Kingdom: Psychology Press.

Baddeley, A. (2003, October). Working memory: Looking back and looking forward. *Nature Reviews Neuroscience, 4*(10), 829–839.

Baddeley, A. D. (2007). *Working memory, thought, and action.* Oxford: Oxford University Press.

Bandura, A. (1986). *Social foundations of thought, and action: A social cognitive theory.* Englewood Cliffs, NJ: Prentice Hall.

Bandura, A. (1997). *Self-efficacy: the exercise of control.* New York: W. H. Freeman.

Barr, A. S. (1958). Characteristics of successful teachers. *Phi Delta Kappan, 39,* 282–284.

Barron, B., & Darling-Hammond, L. (2008). How can we teach for meaningful learning? In L. Darling-Hammond, B. Barron, P. D. Pearson, A. H. Schoenfeld, E. K. Stage, T. D. Zimmerman, G. N. Cervetti, & J. L. Tilson, *Powerful learning: What we know about teaching for understanding* (pp. 11–70). San Francisco: Jossey-Bass.

Baumeister, R. F., & Leary, M. R. (1995). The need to belong: Desire for interpersonal attachments as a fundamental human motivation. *Psychological Bulletin, 117*(3), 497–529.

Beckmann, J., & Heckhausen, H. (2008). Motivation as a function of expectancy and incentive. In J. Heckhausen & H. Heckhausen (Eds.), *Motivation and action* (pp. 99–136). Cambridge: Cambridge University Press.

Bell, N. (2007). *Visualizing and verbalizing.* San Luis Obispo, CA: Gander.

Benard, B. (2005). *What is it about Tribes?* Windsor, CA: CenterSource Systems.

Bhowmik, J. (2013). Enhancing student learning through local and global examples in a statistics unit. *American Journal of Educational Research, 1*(8), 290.

Blakemore, S., & Frith, U. (2005). *The learning brain: Lessons for education.* Malden, MA: Blackwell.

Bloom, B. (1984). *Taxonomy of educational objectives: Book 1. Cognitive domain.* New York: Addison-Wesley. (Originally published in 1956.)

Bradberrry, T., & Greaves, J. (2009). *Emotional intelligence 2.0.* San Diego, CA: TalentSmart.

Brandt, R. (1995, September). Punished by rewards? A conversation with Alfie Kohn. *Educational Leadership.* Available: www.alfiekohn.org/teaching/pbracwak.htm

Bronson, P., & Merryman, A. (2010, July 10). The creativity crisis. *Newsweek.* Available: http://www.newsweek.com/creativity-crisis-74665

Brooks, R., & Goldstein, S. (2008). The mindset of teachers capable of fostering resilience in students. *Canadian Journal of School Psychology, 23,* 114–126.

Brown, S. (2009). *Play: How it shapes the brain, opens the imagination, and invigorates the soul.* New York: Penguin.

Brownell, M. D., Nickel, N. C., Chateau, D., Martens, P. J., Taylor, C., Crockett, L., Katz, A., Sarkar, J., Burland, E., & Gohand, C.Y., the PATHS Equity Team. (2015). Long-term benefits of full-day kindergarten: A longitudinal population-based study. *Early Child Development and Care, 185*:2, 291–316.

Bryk, A. S., & Schneider, B. L. (2002). *Trust in schools: A core resource for improvement.* New York: Russell Sage Foundation.

Burgdorf, J., Wood, P. L., Kroes, R. A., Moskal, J. R., & Panksepp, J. (2007). Neurobiology of 50 kHz ultrasonic vocalizations in rats; Electrode mapping, lesion, and pharmacology studies. *Behavioral Brain Research 182,* 274–283.

Carnegie Mellon University. (n.d.). Students lack interest or motivation. Eberly Center: Teaching Excellence and Educational Innovation. Available: www.cmu.edu/teaching/solveproblem/strat-lackmotivation/lackmotivation-01.html#strat2

Cawelti, G. (Ed.). (2004). *Handbook of research on improving student achievement* (3rd ed.). Princeton, NJ: Editorial Projects in Education.

Center on Education Policy. (2006). *A public education primer: Basic (and sometimes surprising) facts about the U.S. education system.* Washington, DC: Author.

Center on the Developing Child, Harvard University. (n.d.). *InBrief: Executive function: Skills for life and learning.* Cambridge, MA: Author.

Chatham, C. (2007, February 15). Developing intelligence: Dopamine for dummies. Science Blogs. Available: http://scienceblogs.com/developingintelligence/2007/02/15/dopamine-for-dummies

Chen, J. (2008). *Flow in games.* Unpublished master's thesis. Available: www.jenovachen.com/flowingames/Flow_in_games_final.pdf

Chick, N., & Headrick Taylor, K. (2013, March 11). Making student thinking visible: Metacognitive practices in the classroom. Blog, Vanderbilt University, Center for Teaching. Available: http://cft.vanderbilt.edu/2013/03/making-student-thinking -visible-the-impact-of-metacognitive-practice-in-the-classroom

Combs, A. W. (1982). Affective education or none at all. *Educational Leadership, 39*(7), 494–497.

Costa, A., & Kallick, B. (2008). *Learning and leading with habits of mind.* Alexandria, VA: ASCD.

Covili, J. (2012). *Going Google: Powerful tools for 21st century learning.* Thousand Oaks, CA: Corwin.

Crone, E. A., Donohue, S. E., Honomichl, R., Wendelken, C., & Bunge, S. A. (2006). Brain regions mediating flexible rule use during development. *Journal of Neuroscience, 26*(43): 11239–11247.

Csikszentmihalyi, M. (1988). The flow experience and its significance for human psychology. In M. Csikszentmihalyi & I. S. Csikszentmihalyi, *Optimal experience: Psychological studies of flow in consciousness* (pp. 15–35). Cambridge: Cambridge University Press.

Csikszentmihalyi, M., Abuhamdeh, S., & Nakamura, J. (2005). Flow. In A. Elliot (Ed.), *Handbook of competence and motivation* (pp. 598–698). New York: Guilford.

Damasio, A. (2003). *Looking for Spinoza: Joy, sorrow, and the feeling brain.* New York: Harcourt.

Darling-Hammond, L., Austin, K., Cheung, M., & Martin, D. (n.d.). *Thinking about thinking: Metacognition.* Stanford University School of Education, The Learning Classroom Session 9. Available: www.learner.org/courses/learningclassroom/support/09_metacog.pdf

Dean, C. B., Hubbell, E. R., Pitler, H., & Stone, B. (2012). *Classroom instruction that works: Research-based strategies for increasing student achievement* (2nd ed.). Alexandria, VA: ASCD.

de Bono, E. (1994). *de Bono's thinking course* (rev. ed.). New York: Facts on File.

de Bono, E. (1999). *Six thinking hats* (rev. ed.). New York: Little, Brown.

Deci, E. L. (1995). *Why we do what we do: Understanding self-motivation.* New York: Penguin.

Deci, E. L., Koestner, R., & Ryan, R. M. (1999). A meta-analytic review of experiments examining the effects of extrinsic rewards on intrinsic motivation. *Psychological Bulletin, 125,* 627–668.

Deci, E. L., & Ryan, R. M. (1985). *Intrinsic motivation and self-determination in human behavior.* New York: Plenum.

Dennison, P., & Dennison, G. (1992). *Brain Gym: Simple activities for whole-brain learning.* Ventura, CA: Edu Kinesthetics.

Diamond, M., & Hopson, J. (1998). *Magic trees of the mind: How to nurture your child's intelligence, creativity, and healthy emotions from birth through adolescence.* New York: Penguin.

Dickens, C. (1998). *A tale of two cities.* New York: Dover. (Originally published 1859.)

Dolcos, F., LaBar, K. S., & Cabeza, R. (2006). The memory-enhancing effect of emotion: Functional neuroimaging evidence. In B. Uttl, N. Ohta, & A. L. Siegenthaler (Eds.), *Memory and emotion: Interdisciplinary perspectives* (pp. 107–133). Malden, MA: Blackwell.

Drapeau, P. (2014). *Sparking student creativity: Practical ways to promote innovative thinking and problem-solving.* Alexandria, VA: ASCD.

Drubach, D. (2000). *The brain explained.* Upper Saddle River, NJ: Prentice Hall.

Duckworth, A. L., Peterson, C., Matthews, M. D., & Kelly, D. R. (2007). Grit: Perseverance and passion for long-term goals. *Personality Processes and Individual Differences, 92*(6), 1087–1101.

Duckworth, A. L., & Quinn, P. D. (2009). Development and validation of the Short Grit Scale (GRIT–S). *Journal of Personality Assessment, 91*(2), 166–174.

Duncan, G., & Brooks-Gunn, J. (1997). *Consequences of growing up poor.* New York: Russell Sage Foundation.

Dunn, R., & Dunn K. (1987). Dispelling outmoded beliefs about student learning. *Educational Leadership, 44*(6), 55–61.

Dweck, C. (2006). *Mindset: The new psychology of success.* New York: Random House.

Farrington, C. A., Roderick, M., Allensworth, E., Nagaoka, J., Keyes, T. S., Johnson, D. W., & Beechum, N. O. (2012). *Teaching adolescents to become learners. The role of noncognitive factors in shaping school performance: A critical literature review.* Chicago: University of Chicago Consortium on Chicago School Research. Available: https://ccsr.uchicago.edu/sites/default/files/publications/Noncognitive%20Report.pdf

Flavell, J. H. (1979). Metacognition and cognitive monitoring: A new area of cognitive-development inquiry. *American Psychologist, 34,* 906–911.

Foltin, R. W. (2001). Effects of amphetamine, dexfenfluramine, diazepam, and other pharmacological and dietary manipulations on food "seeking" and "taking" behavior in non-human primates. *Psychopharmacology (Berlin), 158,* 28–38.

Fredricks, J. (2014). *Eight myths of student disengagement: Creating classrooms of deep learning.* Thousand Oaks, CA: Corwin.

Fuster, J. (2003). *Cortex and mind: Unifying cognition.* New York: Oxford University Press.

Gallagher, S. A. (1997). Problem-based learning: Where did it come from, what does it do, and where is it going? *Journal for the Education of the Gifted, 20*(4), 332–362.

Galvan, A., Hare, T. A., Parra, C. E., Penn, J., Voss, H., Glover, G., & Casey, B. J. (2006). Earlier development of the accumbens relative to orbitofrontal cortex might underlie risk-taking behavior in adolescents. *Journal of Neuroscience, 26*(25), 6885–5892.

Gardner, H. (2006). *Multiple intelligences: New horizons in history and practice.* New York: Basic Books.

Geake, J. (2009). *The brain at school: Educational neuroscience in the classroom.* Berkshire, UK: McGraw-Hill.

Gee, J. P. (2003). *What video games have to teach us about learning and literacy.* New York: Palgrave Macmillan.

Gibbs, J. (2006). *Reaching all by creating tribes learning communities.* 30th anniversary edition. Windsor, CA: CenterSource Systems.

Glasser, W. (1984). *Control theory in the classroom.* New York: Harper & Row.

Glasser, W. (1990). *Quality school: Managing students without coercion.* New York: Harper & Row.

Glasser, W. (1998). *Choice theory: A new psychology of personal freedom.* New York: HarperCollins.

Glasser, W. (2011). *Take charge of your life: How to get what you need with choice theory psychology.* N.p.: iUniverse.

Goleman, D. (1995). *Emotional intelligence.* New York: Bantam Books.

Good, T. L., & Brophy, J. E. (1995). *Contemporary educational psychology* (5th ed.). White Plains, NY: Longman.

Gopnik, A., Meltzoff, A. N., & Kuhl, P. K. (1999). *The scientist in the crib: Minds, brains, and how children learn.* New York: Morrow.

Grandin, T. (2010). *Animals make us human: Creating the best life for animals.* New York: Mariner Books.

Green, E. J., Greenough, W. T., & Schlumpf, B. E. (1983). Effects of complex or isolated environments on cortical dendrites of middle-aged rats. *Brain Research, 264,* 233–240.

Gregorc, A. (1982). *Inside styles: Beyond the basics.* Columbia, CT: Gregorc Associates.

Gregory, G. H. (2005). *Differentiating instruction with style.* Thousand Oaks, CA: Corwin.

Gregory, G. H. (2013). *Differentiated instructional strategies for professional development.* Thousand Oaks, CA: Corwin.

Gregory, G. H., & Chapman, C. (2013). *Differentiated instructional strategies: One size doesn't fit all* (3rd ed.). Thousand Oaks, CA: Corwin.

Gregory, G. H., & Kaufeldt, M. (2012). *Think big, start small: How to differentiate instruction in a brain-friendly classroom.* Bloomington, IN: Solution Tree.

Griggs, J., & Walker, R. (2008). *The costs of child poverty for individuals and society: A literature review.* York, England: Joseph Rowntree.

Hallowell, E. M. (2011). *Shine: Using brain science to get the best from your people.* Boston: Harvard Business Review Press.

Hanson, J. R., & Silver, H. F. (1978). *Learning styles and strategies.* Moorestown, NJ: Hanson Silver Strong.

Harmin, M., & Toth, M. (2006). *Inspiring active learning: A complete handbook for today's teachers.* Alexandria, VA: ASCD.

Hart, L. (1981, March). Brain, language, and new concepts of learning. *Educational Leadership,* pp. 443–445.

Hart, L. (1983). *Human brain and human learning.* New York: Longman.

Hattie, J. (2009). *Visible learning.* New York: Routledge Academic.

Hattie, J., & Yates, G. (2014). *Visible learning and the science of how we learn.* New York: Routledge Academic.

Haystead, M. W., & Marzano, R. J. (2009). *Meta-analytic synthesis of studies conducted at Marzano Research Laboratory on instructional strategies.* Englewood, CO: Marzano Research Laboratory.

Hebb, D. O. (1949/2002). *The organization of behavior: A neuropsychological theory.* Mahwah, NJ: Erlbaum.

Hennenlotter, A., Schroeder, U., Erhard, P., Castrop, F., Haslinger, B., Stoecker, D., Lange, K. W., & Ceballos-Baumann, A. O. (2005). A common neural basis for receptive and expressive communication of pleasant facial affect. *Neuroimage, 26,* 581–591.

Hennessey, B. A., & Amabile, T. M. (1987) *Creativity and Learning.* Washington, DC: National Education Association.

Herd, S., Mingus, B., O'Reilly, R. (n.d.). *Dopamine and self-directed learning.* Unpublished paper, Department of Psychology and Neuroscience, University of Colorado, 345 UCB, Boulder, CO.

Hernández, R. S., & Gay, G. (1996). Student perceptions of disciplinary conflict in ethnically diverse classrooms. *NASSP Bulletin, 80*(580), 84–94.

Hofstadter, D., & Sander, E. (2013). *Surfaces and essences: Analogy as the fuel and fire of thinking.* New York: Basic Books.

Johnson, D., Johnson, R., & Holubec, E. (1998). *Cooperation in the classroom.* Edina, MN: Interaction.

Johnson, D. W., & Johnson, R. (1981). Effects of cooperative and individualistic learning experiences on interethnic interaction. *Journal of Educational Psychology, 73,* 454–459.

Jones, C. (1994). *Mistakes that worked: 40 inventions and how they came to be.* New York: Delacorte.

Jones, F. (2013). *Tools for reaching* (3rd ed.). Santa Cruz, CA: Fredrick H. Jones & Associates.

Kandel, E. (2006). *In search of memory: The emergence of a new science of mind.* New York: Norton.

Kaplan, F., & Oudeyer, P. Y. (2007, November). In search of the neural circuits of intrinsic motivation. *Frontiers in Neuroscience, 1*(1), 225–236. Available: www.ncbi.nlm.nih.gov/pmc/articles/PMC2518057

Kember, D., Ho, A., & Hong, C. (2008, November). The importance of establishing relevance in motivating student learning. *Active Learning in Higher Education, 9*(3), 249–263.

Kenny, N. (2010, April 30). Relevance: The secret to motivate student learning. Blog. Available: http://natashakenny.wordpress.com/2010/04/30/relevance-the-secret-to-motivating-student-learning

Kim, K. H. (2012, July 10). "Yes, there *is* a creativity crisis!" The Creativity Post. Available: www.creativitypost.com/education/yes_there_is_a_creativity_crisis#sthash.HA41cZyU.dpuf

Knowles, M. S. (1975). *Self-directed learning: A guide for learners and teachers.* Englewood Cliffs, NJ: Prentice Hall.

Kohn, A. (1999). *Punished by rewards.* Boston: Houghton Mifflin.

Kohn, A. (2004, November). Challenging students . . . and how to have more of them. *Phi Delta Kappan.* Available: www.alfiekohn.org/teaching/challenging.htm

Kohn, A. (2014a, September 9). Dispelling the myth of deferred gratification: What waiting for a marshmallow doesn't prove. *Education Week.* Available: www.edweek.org/ew/articles/2014/09/09/03kohn.h34.html

Kohn, A. (2014b). The myth of the spoiled child: Challenging the conventional wisdom about children and parenting. *Education Week, 34*(3), 25, 28, 32.

Larmer, J. (2014, June 30). Grit happens in PBL. Edutopia blog. Available: www.edutopia.org/blog/grit-happens-in-pbl-john-larmer

Lopez, J. (2013). *Handbook of positive psychology.* Oxford: Oxford University Press.

Lou, Y., Abrami, P. C., & d'Apollonia, S. (2001). Small group and individual learning with technology: A meta-analysis, *Review of Educational Research, 71*(3), 449–521.

Lou, Y., Abrami, P. C., Spence, J. C., Paulsen, C., Chambers, B., & d'Apollonio, S. (1996). Within-class grouping: A meta-analysis. *Review of Educational Research, 66*(4), 423–458.

Louv, R. (2005). *Last child in the woods: Saving our children from nature deficit disorder.* New York: Algonquin Books.

Lyman, F., & McTighe, J. (1988, April). Cueing thinking in the classroom: The promise of theory-embedded tools. *Educational Leadership,* p. 7.

Marzano, R. (2010, February). Meeting students where they are. *Education Leadership, 67*(5), 71–72.

Marzano, R. J., Pickering, D. J., & Pollock, J. E. (2001). *Classroom instruction that works: Research-based strategies for increasing student achievement.* Alexandria, VA: ASCD.

Maslow, A. (1968). *Toward a psychology of being* (2nd ed.). New York: Van Nostrand.

McCombs, B. L., & Whisler, J. S. (1997). *The learner-centered classroom and school.* San Francisco: Jossey-Bass.

McLeod, S. A. (2008). Peterson and Peterson, 1959. Retrieved from http://www .simplypsychology.org/peterson-peterson.html

McNerney, S. (2012, May 31). What motivates creativity. Available: http://bigthink .com/insights-of-genius/what-motivates-creativity.

McTighe, J., & Wiggins, G. (2013). *Essential questions: Opening doors to student understanding.* Alexandria, VA: ASCD.

Middleton, M., & Perks, K. (2014). *Motivation to learn: Transforming classroom culture to support student achievement.* Thousand Oaks, CA: Corwin.

Mitra, S. (2013, February). *Build a school in the cloud.* TED2013 presentation. Available: www.ted.com/talks/sugata_mitra_build_a_school_in_the_cloud

Morehead, J. (2012, June 9). Stanford University's Carol Dweck on the growth mindset and education. OneDublin.org. Available: http://onedublin.org/2012/06/19/stanford-universitys-carol-dweck-on-the-growth-mindset-and-education/

Murphy, C. (2011). *Why games work and the science of learning.* Paper presented at the 19th International Congress on Modeling and Simulation, Perth, Australia.

Nakamura, J., & Csikszentmihalyi, M. (2001). Flow theory and research. In C. R. Snyder, E. Wright, & S. J. Lopez (Eds.), *Handbook of positive psychology* (pp. 195–206). Oxford: Oxford University Press.

National Center for Education Statistics. (2002). *Digest for education statistics tables and figures.* Washington, DC: U.S. Government Printing Office. Available: http:// nces.ed.gov/programs/digest/d02/dt066.asp

National Center for Education Statistics. (2005). *Digest for education statistics tables and figures.* Washington, DC: U.S. Government Printing Office. Available: http:// nces.edu.gov/programs/d05/tables/dt05_038.asp

National Research Council. (2000). *How people learn.* Washington, DC: National Academies Press.

National Research Council, & Institute of Medicine. (2003). *Engaging schools: Fostering high school students' motivation to learn.* Washington, DC: National Academies Press.

National Scientific Council on the Developing Child, Harvard University. (2007, January). *The science of early childhood development: Closing the gap between what we know and what we do.* Cambridge, MA: Author.

Niemiec, C. P., Ryan, R. M., & Deci, E. L. (2009). The path taken: Consequences of attaining intrinsic and extrinsic aspirations in post-college life. *Journal of Research in Personality, 43*(3), 291–306.

Nieoullon, A., & Coquerel, A. (2003, December). Dopamine: A key regulator to adapt action, emotion, motivation and cognition. *Current Opinions in Neurology, 16*(Suppl. 2), S3–S9.

Nieto, S. (1996). *Affirming diversity: The sociopolitical context of education.* White Plains, NY: Longman.

O'Doherty, J. P. (2004). Reward representations and reward-related learning in the human brain: Insight from neuroimaging. *Current Opinion in Neurobiology, 14,* 769–776.

Panksepp, J. (1998). *Affective neuroscience: The foundations of human and animal emotions.* New York: Oxford University Press.

Panksepp, J., & Biven, L. (2012). *The archaeology of mind: Neuroevolutionary origins of human emotions.* New York: Norton.

Panksepp, J., Siviy, S., & Normansell, L. A. (1984). The psychology of play: Theoretical and methodological perspectives. *Neuroscience and Biobehavioral Reviews, 8(4),* pp. 465–492.

Partnership for 21st Century Skills. (n.d.). *Learning for the 21st century: A report and MILE guide for 21st century skills.* Washington, DC: Author. Available: www .p21.org/storage/documents/P21_Report.pdf

Pecina, S., & Berridge, K. (2013). Dopamine or opioid stimulation of nucleus accumbens similarly amplify cue-triggered "wanting" for reward. *European Journal of Neuroscience, 37,* 1529–1540.

Philpot, R. M., McQuown, S., & Kirstein, C. L. (2001). Stereotaxic localization of the developing nucleus accumbens septi. *Brain Research, 130*(1), 149–153.

Pink, D. (2009). *Drive: The surprising truth about what motivates us.* New York: Riverhead Books.

Plato. (n.d. /2009). *The republic* (B. Jowett, Trans.) Thousand Oaks, CA: BN Publishing.

Prensky, M. (2010). *Teaching digital natives: Partnering for real learning.* Thousand Oaks, CA: Corwin.

Pritchard, R., & Ashwood, E. (2008). *Managing motivation: A manager's guide to diagnosing and improving motivation.* New York: Routledge Academic.

Pritscher, C. P. (2011). *Brains inventing themselves.* Amsterdam: Sense Publishers. Available: www.sensepublishers.com/media/121-brains-inventing-themselves.pdf

Quaglia, R. J., & Corso, M. J. (2014). *Student voice: The instrument of change.* Thousand Oaks, CA: Corwin.

Ratey, J. J. (2008). *Spark: The revolutionary new science of exercise and the brain.* New York: Little, Brown.

Raz, A., & Buhle, J. (2006). Typologies of attentional networks. *Nature Reviews Neuroscience, 7,* 367–379.

Resnick, L., & Klopfer, L. E. (Eds.) (1989). *Toward the thinking curriculum: Current cognitive research.* Alexandria, VA: ASCD.

Robinson, K. (2009). *The element: How finding your passion changes everything.* New York: Penguin Books.

Rutledge, P. (2012, August 28). The positive side of video games: Part III. Media Psychology blog. Available: http://pamelarutledge.com/media_psychology/video-games?print=pdf-page

Salamone, J. D. (1992). Complex motor and sensorimotor functions of striatal and accumbens dopamine: Involvement in instrumental behavior processes. *Psychopharmacology (Berlin) 107*, 160–174.

Salamone, J. D. (1994). The involvement of nucleus accumbens dopamine in appetitive and aversive motivation. *Behavioral Brain Research, 61*, 117–133.

Salamone, J. D. (2010). Motor function and motivation. In G. Koob, M. Le Moal, R. F. Thompson (Eds.), *Encyclopedia of Behavioral Neuroscience, Volume 3*. Academic Press, Oxford (2010), pp. 267–276.

Salamone, J. D., & Correa, M. (2002). Motivational views of reinforcement: Implications for understanding the behavioral functions of nucleus accumbens dopamine. *Behavioral Brain Research, 137*, 3–25.

Saltzman, A. (2010). *Mindfulness: A teacher's guide.* Available: www.pbs.org/thebuddha/teachers-guide

Sapolsky, R. M. (1998). *Why zebras don't get ulcers.* New York: Freeman.

Saxena, S. (2013, November 14). How can technology enhance student creativity? *EdTechReview,* INSIGHT Blog. Available: http://edtechreview.in/trends-insights/insights/750-how-can-technology-enhance-student-creativity

Schaffer, O. (2013). *Crafting fun user experiences: A method to facilitate flow.* Fairfield, IA: Human Factors International.

Schopenhauer, W. (1999). *Prize essay on the freedom of the will.* Cambridge Texts in the History of Philosophy, G. Zoller (Ed.) and E. F. J. Payne (Trans.). Cambridge: Cambridge University Press.

Schunk, D. H. (1989). Self-efficacy and achievement behaviors. *Educational Psychology Review, 1*, 173–208.

Shachar, H., & Sharon, S. (1994). Talking, relating, and achieving: Effects of cooperative learning circles. *Instructional Science, 19*, 445–466.

Shechtman, N., DeBarger, A. H., Dornsife, C., et al. (Eds.). (2013). *Promoting grit, tenacity, and perseverance: Critical factors for success in the 21st century.* Washington, DC: U.S. Department of Education, Office of Educational Technology. Available: http://pgbovine.net/OET-Draft-Grit-Report-2-17-13.pdf

Sheets, R. H., & Gay, G. (1996, May). Student perceptions of disciplinary conflict in ethnically diverse classrooms. *NASSP Bulletin*, pp. 84–93.

Silver, H., Strong, R., & Perini, M. (2000). *So each may learn: Integrating learning styles and multiple intelligences.* Alexandria, VA: ASCD.

Slavin, R. E. (1990). *Cooperative learning: Theory, research, and practice.* Englewood Cliffs, NJ: Prentice Hall.

Snyder, C. R., & Lopez, S. J. (2007). *Positive psychology: The scientific and practical explorations of human strengths.* London: Sage.

Solms, M., & Panksepp, J. (2012). The "id" knows more than the "ego" admits: Neuropsychoanalytic and primal consciousness perspectives on the interface between affective and cognitive neuroscience. *Brain Sciences, 2*, 147–175.

Sousa, D. A. (2010). *Mind, brain, and education: Neuroscience implications for the classroom—Leading Edge Book 6.* Bloomington, IN: Solution Tree.

Sousa, D. A., & Tomlinson, C. A. (2011). *Differentiation and the brain: How neuroscience supports the learner friendly classroom.* Bloomington, IN: Solution Tree.

Stepien, W., Gallagher, S., & Workman, D. (1993). Problem-based learning for traditional and interdisciplinary classrooms. *Journal for Gifted Education, 16,* 338–357.

Sternberg, R. (1996). *Successful intelligence: How practical and creative intelligence determine success in life.* New York: Simon & Schuster.

Stiggins, R. (1993a, May 5). Authentic Assessment workshop presented at the Train the Trainers conference, Toronto, Canada.

Stiggins, R. (1993b). *Student-centered classroom assessment.* Englewood Cliffs, NJ: Prentice Hall.

Stiggins, R. J. (2001). *Student-involved classroom assessment* (3rd ed.). Upper Saddle River, NJ: Merrill/Prentice Hall.

Storm, E., & Tecott, L. H. (2005). Social circuits: Peptidergic regulation of mammalian social behavior. *Neuron, 47*(4), 483–486.

Sutherland, K. S., & Oswald, D. (2005). The relationship between teacher and student behavior in classrooms for students with EBD: Transactional processes. *Journal of Child and Family Studies, 14,* 1–14.

Sylwester, R., & D. Moursund (Eds.). (2014). *Understanding and mastering complexity.* Eugene, OR: Information Age Education.

Thorndike, E. (1932). *The fundamentals of learning.* New York: AMS Press.

Tortora, G., & Grabowski, S. (1996). *Principles of anatomy and physiology* (8th ed.). New York: HarperCollins.

Tough, P. (2011, September 14). What if the secret to success is failure? *New York Times.* Available: www.nytimes.com/2011/09/18/magazine/what-if-the-secret-to-success-is-failure.html

Tough, P. (2012). *How children succeed: Grit, curiosity, and the hidden power of character.* New York: Houghton Mifflin.

Trilling, B., & Fadel, C. (2009). *21st century skills: Learning for life in our times.* San Francisco: Jossey-Bass.

Tulving, E., & Craik, F. I. M. (Eds.). (2000). *The Oxford handbook of memory.* London: Oxford University Press.

Vandekerckhove, M., Bulnes, L. C., & Panksepp, J. (2014, January 3). Emergence of primary anoetic consciousness in episodic memory. *Frontiers in Behavioral Neuroscience, 7*(210).

Villegas, A. M., & Lucas, T. (2002). *Educating culturally responsive teachers: A coherent approach.* Albany, NY: SUNY Press.

Vygotsky, L. S. (1978). *Mind in society: The development of higher psychological processes.* Cambridge, MA: Harvard University Press.

Wagner, T. (2008a). *The global achievement gap: Why even our best schools don't teach the new survival skills our children need—and what we can do about it.* New York: Basic Books.

Wagner, T. (2008b, October). Rigor redefined. *Educational Leadership, 66*(2), 20–25.

Wang, J., Rao, H., Wetmore, G. S., Furlan, P. M., Korczykowski, M., Dinges, D. F., et al. (2005). Perfusion functional MRI reveals cerebral blood flow pattern under psychological stress. *Proceedings of the National Academy of Sciences of the United States of America, 102,* 17804–17809.

Wasserman, H., & Danforth, H. E. (1988). *The human bond: Support groups and mutual aid.* New York: Springer.

Watson, J. B. (1930). *Behaviorism* (rev. ed.). Chicago: University of Chicago Press.

Webb, N. L. (2002, March 28). *Depth-of-knowledge levels for four content areas.* Unpublished paper.

Weintraub, P. (May 31, 2012). Discover interview: Jaak Panksepp pinned down humanity's 7 primal emotions. *Discover.* Retrieved from: http://discovermagazine .com/2012/may/11-jaak-panksepp-rat-tickler-found-humans-7-primal-emotions

White, H. (1995). "Creating problems" for PBL. Available: www.udel.edu/pbl/cte/ jan95-chem.html

Wiggins, G., & McTighe, J. (1998). *Understanding by design.* Alexandria, VA: ASCD.

Wikipedia contributors. (2011). Creativity and motivation: Are creativity and intelligence related? *Wikipedia, The Free Encyclopedia* http://creativitytheories .wikispaces.com/Creativity+and+Motivation.

Wikipedia contributors. (n.d.). Incentive salience. *Wikipedia, The Free Encyclopedia,* http://en.wikipedia.org/wiki/Incentive-salience

Willis, J. (2008). *How your child learns best: Brain-friendly strategies you can use to ignite your child's learning and increase school success.* Naperville, IL: Sourcebooks.

Willis, J. (2010, May 9). Want children to "pay attention"? Make their brains curious! *Psychology Today.* Available: www.psychologytoday.com/blog/radical -teaching/201005/want-children-pay-attention-make-their-brains-curious

Winne, P. H., & Hadwin, A. F. (2008). The weave of motivation and self-regulated learning. In D. H. Schunk & B. J. Zimmerman, *Motivation and self-regulated Learning: Theory, research, and application* (pp. 297–314). New York: Routledge.

Wright, J. S., & Panksepp, J. (2012). An evolutionary framework to understand foraging, wanting, and desire: The neuropsychology of the SEEKING system. *Neuropsychoanalysis, 14*(1).

Yerkes, R. M., & Dodson, J. D. (2007). The relation of strength of stimulus to rapidity of habit-formation. In D. Smith, M. Bar-Eli, D. Smith, & M. Bar-Eli (Eds.), *Essential readings in sport and exercise psychology* (pp. 13–22). Champaign, IL: Human Kinetics.

Young, P. T. (1961). *Motivation and emotion.* New York: Wiley.

Zatorre, R. J. & Salimpoora, V. N. (2013). From perception to pleasure: Music and its neural substrates. *Proceedings of the National Academies of Sciences, 110* (Suppl 2): 10430–10437.

Index

Note: Page numbers followed by an italicized *f* indicate information in figures.

About the Authors

Gayle Gregory is an internationally known consultant who has specialized in brain compatible learning and differentiated instruction and assessment. She presents practical teacher- and student-friendly strategies grounded in sound research that educators find easy to use in the classroom or schoolhouse tomorrow. Her interactive style and modeling of strategies help teachers and administrators transfer new ideas with ease.

Gayle has had extensive experience in elementary, middle, and secondary schools, community colleges, and universities. She has also had district leadership roles including curriculum coordinator and staff development director. Gayle has worked with Instructional Leadership Teams in many schools and districts throughout the country focusing on data analysis using both formative and summative assessment; and differentiating instruction based on readiness, learning profiles, and interests.

Gayle's areas of expertise include brain-compatible learning, block scheduling, emotional intelligence, instructional and assessment practices, differentiated instructional strategies, using data to differentiate, literacy, presentation skills, renewal of secondary schools, enhancing teacher quality, coaching and mentoring, managing change, and building professional learning communities.

Gayle is the author and coauthor of numerous publications for teachers and administrators. She may be contacted through gaylegregory@netscape.net or www.gaylegregory.com.

 **Martha Kaufeldt** is a full-time trainer and consultant with an extensive background in brain-compatible teaching and learning. She has taught at all grade levels, served as a district-level gifted coordinator and staff developer, and was the lead teacher and restructuring coordinator of a demonstration "brain-compatible" school.

Martha is a popular trainer and keynoter for individual schools, districts, and institutes, as well as for international educational conferences. She gives motivational presentations and dynamic workshops throughout the United States and Canada that address the fundamentals of brain compatible learning, differentiated instruction, and integrated curriculum for all grade levels.

Martha served as the program director, trainer, and coach for the Bay Area Middle Schools Project. In five years, the project trained and coached more than 300 teachers and administrators to use the strategies that can assist schools in beginning the difficult process of total restructuring. When her schedule allows, Martha frequently returns to the middle school classroom to get a "reality check." As a 7th grade Humanities Core teacher, Martha was able to work on an interdisciplinary teaching team implementing thematic curriculum, as well as being at a school beginning the restructuring process. As a new challenge Martha then worked for four years as the restructuring coordinator and the lead teacher at an alternative K–6 public elementary school in Santa Cruz, California. This demonstration program emphasizes brain compatible teaching strategies, thematic integrated curriculum, multiage classes, authentic assessment, parent participation, and conflict resolution strategies. Martha now works as a consulting teacher for a public charter school in Felton, CA. She is a strong advocate for integrating collaboration, movement, discovery play, and